Called to Parent:

How to Live the Abundant Life While Single Parenting

Ranè Monique, M.Div.

Love and Faith Publishing
Indianapolis, IN

ISBN: 9781709738159

Printed in the United States of America

Cover Design: Alyssa Banks

Love and Faith Publishing
Indianapolis, IN
RevRane@Yahoo.com

Dedication

This book is dedicated to My Heavenly Father, The Most Excellent Single Parent of all. Also, to my wonderful son, General Jaire Lynch, "Jai," who has allowed me to get it wrong a time or two. And, last but not least, my loving parents, Raymond and Rhonda Lynn, who built the foundation on which I stand.

Table of Contents

Foreword

For most of my life my mom has been a minister. So, that pretty much tells you that I was raised in the church. Every Sunday and most Wednesdays we were there. I accepted God in my life at an early age because I saw how He was working in my mother's life and that made me want to get baptized and give my life to Christ.

My mom has always challenged me to do better, not only academically, but also with sports and anything else I pursued. She pushed me to do what I didn't know I could do. I'm thankful for that.

She has always had such high expectations of me, which I hated, because it put a lot of pressure on me. In school if I made a "C," she would always say "you can do better if you apply yourself, just apply yourself." I can still hear her saying that to me.

Being raised by a single mother and not having my dad in the home was difficult. Although he was always there when I called, I wanted him in the home with me. When I got in trouble or found myself needing help, I really wish he was there, because you just can't talk to women about everything.

My mom would always call my father to be a part of the discussion, but I don't think it was really as effective as actual in-home parenting. All in all, I know that both of my parents love me and I wouldn't be the young man that I am today without them.

I'm proud of my mom and all that she has accomplished. I hope that kids living in a single parent household will see an improvement in their home life. I hope that families will enjoy each other more because of this book. My mother has a lot of wisdom and compassion. She's shared it with me over the years. Hopefully, you are able to glean a portion of what I've gotten from this great woman of God, My Mom.

General J. Lynch

Introduction:

The Gazelle, Fawn & Wild Dog

In 2011, I traveled to Kenya, Africa with fellow classmates of Christian Theological Seminary in Indianapolis, Indiana. For about two weeks we journeyed on an excursion learning about the culture and history of the Kenyan people. We traveled to Nairobi, Eldoret, visited the Great Rift Valley and several other monuments and cities in between.

Upon arrival to the country we ventured to one of the largest tea plantations in the town of Limuru, where tea was first introduced to the Kenyans. There, we learned interesting facts about tea- harvesting (plucking) and manufacturing. We also met with those who lived and worked on the plantation and had our first interaction with monkeys, while there.

One day, while simply riding through a rural town, we observed a herd of zebras migrating to the Serengeti. About 30 of them crossed the street right in front of our van. I saw, in that moment, more zebras than I'd ever seen in all the zoos, combined, in the United States. It was an amazing sight to behold.

More than that, we had a wonderful opportunity to spend the weekend in luxury tents near Maasai Mara, the safari we would later venture on. I was most excited about that. I'd seen that kind of thing many times on television and on the internet, but the pictures and videos hardly did it any justice.

The safari, itself, was nothing short of amazing. We witnessed, firsthand, lions mating and even a lioness hunting a wildebeest. We saw the "Big 5" animals of Massai Mara- the lion, rhino, elephant, buffalo and the leopard. I found a porcupine quill while eating my lunch, picnic-style, in the wild. And, I saw in their original habitat, my favorite African animal, the hippopotamus. As a bonus, we had the opportunity to socialize with and be 'baptized' by members of the Maasai Warriors, Kenya's most notable tribe of indigenous people.

As exciting as the aforementioned was, it would be the *journey to the safari* that has greatly influenced my views on parenting and prompted my writing this book. One simple act of nature- an interaction between a wild dog, a gazelle and her fawn has given me a better understanding of what it means to "train your child(ren) in the way that they should go."[1]

Although these were certainly not the safari animals I was anticipating, I was very much captivated by the encounter, *my own National Geographic moment*. For I was observing nature in real time, this time, and not on television.

Driving along the plane, on the way to the safari, I observed a wild dog chasing a gazelle and baby fawn... at least that was my initial thought. However, it quickly became clear that the wild dog's intentions were undeniably for the fawn and not the gazelle, for the gazelle was no force to be reckoned with.

Whenever the wild dog got near the fawn, the gazelle would head-butt the wild dog and knock it off its' feet, allowing the fawn to escape. The gazelle embodied so much strength and courage that the wild dog, her predator, didn't stand a chance. I remember thinking, "Female gazelles have mama strength, LOL," the kind that protects her child by any means necessary.

This cycle (dog getting close to fawn, gazelle intervening by head-butting the dog) continued as we drove along the plain. At one point, I thought to myself, "surely the gazelle could just defeat the wild dog seeing her ability to knock him off his feet time and time again." I thought, "Why doesn't she just destroy this threat to her fawn? Why was she tolerating the wild dog's attack?"

The answer to those questions lie-in the invaluable lesson I learned that day about parenting. Parents can't always "destroy" the threats and attacks that exist in the world or that come for our children. We can only discipline and provide our kids with the necessary tools that they need to survive the 'attacks of the enemy.' The gazelle was simply training her fawn to survive.

We, too, have to train and equip our kids with the tools they need to survive the wild. We have to help them understand and utilize their potential and power so that they, too, can run with fidelity the race of life.

We also have to be invested in our children and the call to parent. If we are to live the abundant life God has for us, we must learn how to parent God's Way. For, parenting is no easy feat and single parenting is even harder. But, with the help of the Lord, discipline and perseverance, we can raise happy, healthy kids who love God while enjoying the abundant life God has for us.

Chapter 1: *Human Nature*

"The temptations in your life are no different from what others experience. And God is faithful. He will not allow the temptation to be more than you can stand.

When you are tempted, He will show you a way out so that you can endure."

1 Corinthians 10:13, NLT

When it comes to single parenting, I have the tendency to be more reactive to situations than I am proactive. And, even when I think I'm proactive, it's usually counterproductive, lol. I often wonder how much easier it would be if parenting came with a user's manual, an answer key or some kind of guide to help navigate the way. Because parenting is hard work and single parenting, even harder!

Single parenting is like living in a science lab, constantly working on a HUGE EXPERIMENT full of assumptions, observations, guinea pigs, RATS, combustions, explosions and... victories. One day you're on top of the world and the next day the world's on top of you. Seems you take two steps forward to take ten steps back. "O wretched man (woman) that I am! Who will deliver me from this body of sin and death?"₁ LOL.

Seriously, parenting has a way of bringing out the good and bad in us all. It exposes *many* of our strengths and ALL of our weaknesses. You don't know just how messed up you really are until you have kids. LOL.

There have been numerous times I've felt like I was failing as a parent; failing both my child and God. I would say the wrong things, fail to acknowledge successes, and on many days, forget to stop and smell the roses, LITERALLY.

I remember when my son, Jai, was about three or four years old, he would pick dandelions and bring them to me. At first it was so cute and it really touched my heart, but then it became excessive, I thought. I don't know why it was such a nuisance to me, but I eventually made him stop picking them altogether. He's seventeen now... oh, how I wish he'd pick me a dandelion.

Single parenting?! Yeah, I've blown it... A lot! But, God has strategically connected me with people who understand my plight and are willing to come alongside this endeavor. It has been a blessing to have these people in our lives because so often single parents think our situations are isolated and rare. We think we're the only ones going through whatever it is that we are going through. But, that's not case. We are never alone.

When we commune with other single parents we learn that although our stories range in complexity and severity, they are very much similar in nature. For "there is nothing new under the sun."2 Understanding this has helped me to better navigate the ups and downs and the ins and outs of single parenting.

Through talking with other parents, I have found that our life stories mirror the lives of many people we read about in the Bible today. The frailty of humankind, love and war, passion, the ability to choose and the destructive patterns that plague us all, are all found in the narratives of the Bible.

More importantly, we find in Scripture a Wise, Loving, Merciful God, Who is always Faithful & Gracious to us all. It's this truth about God that has empowered me to get up time and time again when life has knocked me down and challenged my single parenting. It's my hope that you, too, will find assurance in these stories and that you will know you are not alone. God is Faithful and He will continue to be Faithful to you and your children.

Adam & Eve

I find it most befitting to begin with the parents of all parents, Adam and Eve, whose story we read about in Genesis 2-4. Adam and Eve were living in pure (marital) bliss when the serpent (the devil) tempted Eve to eat from the forbidden *Tree of the Knowledge of Good and Evil*.3 "She then gave fruit to her husband and he also ate."4 Their actions were so detestable to God that they found themselves banished from paradise. They learned firsthand what it meant to live outside of the will of God and under a curse.

Where they once walked with God and enjoyed the glamorous life, they were now outcasts living in hostility. You see, in the Garden there was no sin. Nothing impure. Nothing wrong. Nothing missing. They had what scripture refers to as the "fullness of joy."5 But, they forfeited paradise for a moment of pleasure. They sinned against God and were driven from the Garden.

Once banished from the Garden of Eden, they went on to birth two sons, Cain and Abel. Cain, we are told, was the older son and a gardener. Abel, the youngest, attended the flock.6

Now, God required a sacrifice from humanity as restitution for sin, after the fall of Adam and Eve. The Word tells us that Cain brought the Lord "some of the fruits of the soil," on occasion.7 Abel, on the other hand, brought the Lord a "fat offering of the firstborn of his flock."8 According to Genesis 4, "The Lord looked with favor upon Abel and his offering, but on Cain and his offering, He did not look with favor."9 This infuriated Cain and he determined in his heart to murder his younger brother, Abel.10 He was jealous of him.

Cain, we see, also had an anger management issue, for he threw a temper tantrum that resulted in murder. God said to Cain when He perceived what was in his heart, "Why are you angry? Why is your face downcast? If you do what is right, will you not be accepted? But if you do not do what is right, sin is crouching at your door; it desires to have you, but you must master it."11 God was trying to work with Cain, but Cain was defiant. He left the presence of God and went out to murder Abel.

Cain's anger issues originally stemmed from Ada and Eve's disobedience to God. When Adam and Eve defied God in the Garden of Eden, they opened the door for all manner of sin to enter their children's lives. It was *their sin* that prompted it, for the Word tells us that "through Adam sin entered the world."[12] It is the ~~result~~ *effect* of Adam's disobedience that still plagues families today. "But, thanks be to God, who has given us the power to triumph"[13] over this *original sin*.

Sarah, Abraham & Hagar

The Bible is filled with jaw-dropping, eyes-widening, on the edge of your seat narratives. And, the story of Abraham and Sarah found in the book of Genesis is one of the most dramatic & captivating stories of them all. It's a story of love, an extra-marital affair, betrayal and blessings.

Abraham, coined by God as the "Father of Many Nations," is highly revered as the forefather of the three major religions- Judaism, Christianity and Islam.[14] He was given this title for his willingness to trust in the One True God, Jehovah. Before that time, Abraham and all the people of the world were polytheistic, believing in multiple gods.

One day, God met with Abraham to share the good news that he and his wife, Sarah, would have a son. This didn't occur right away, however. In fact, God took many years to deliver on this promise and Abraham and Sarah were both senior citizens anyway. So, the impatient Sarah conjured up a plan to take matters into her own hands... well, she put the matter into her husband's hands, if you will, lol.

Sarah decided that God needed to birth her child through Hagar, her maid servant. Her plan went forth and Abraham and Sarah (through Hagar) conceived a son, Ishmael. In Antiquity, the maidservant and all the help were property of the owner. Because Hagar belonged to Sarah, Hagar's child belonged to Sarah. Therefore, Sarah and Abraham raised Ishmael as their own while Hagar continued to serve Sarah and to care for the child.

The Bible says that before Ishmael was born, Hagar started feeling herself. [15]Since she was carrying her mistresses' husband's baby, lol, she started to "despise" Sarah, and Sarah was fed up with Maidservant Hagar. It got so bad between the two women that Sarah forced Hagar to flee the camp.[16]

Hagar ran away from her abusive mistress, Sarah, but "the angel of the Lord *found* (her) near a spring in the desert" and blessed her.[17] This is astounding for two reasons: (1) it's unusual to find springs of water in the desert, suggesting God created the spring of water exclusively for a parched and pregnant Hagar and (2) God blessed Hagar although she was not privy to the blessing because she was a slave.

Let's take into consideration Hagar's feelings when the Lord *found* her. She was forced to marry and conceive a child that was no longer her own, she was ridiculed by her mistress, and would be an outcast to her family if she dared to return home. I'm certain that she felt used and abused. She was lonely and had nowhere to go. But God!

God promised to bless Hagar in spite of her situation. He said, "I will so increase your descendants that they will be too numerous to count."[18] Now, that may not sound like good news today, but, technically, it was a blessing and not a curse in antiquity, lol.

God wants you to know that in spite of your current situation- who you are, how you were conceived, how your children were conceived... whether through extra-marital affairs, a one-night stand or IVF, He loves you! He promises to be "with you always, even to the end of the world," just like he was there for Hagar.[19] God knows how to make any situation work for our good.[20] He's God and He's just good like that.

Lot & Family

The story of Lot and his family centers around a very sensitive issue that affects so many families still today. Found in Genesis 19 in the ancient cities of Sodom and Gomorrah, this story depicts a family living amongst all manner of evil... things which were an abomination to God. Because of this evil, God planned to destroy the cities. Abraham pleaded with God to have mercy on the cities because his nephew Lot lived there.[21] God had mercy on Lot and his family and sent angels in the form of men to rescue them from the impending doom. But, when the men of God entered Sodom, they encountered opposition from Lot, himself.

The men of God wanted to survey the scene but Lot derailed them, for he was a gatekeeper.[22] A gatekeeper is someone with the authority to allow or deny entrance into a city or place. They control who or what enters and leaves the city.

Lot suggested that the men stay at his home instead of venturing out into the cities. He didn't want to expose them to the wickedness occurring there... as if they didn't already know. They obliged to stay with him.

That evening, the men of Sodom surrounded Lot's house demanding to have sex with the men of God. They wanted to rape them. 23

Sodom means "a very sinful, corrupt, vice-ridden place."24 Jude 1:7 describes Sodom and Gomorrah as being "filled with immorality and every kind of sexual perversion." The people's lifestyle was an abomination to God. This was the kind of lifestyle that Lot allowed into the city, the kind of lifestyle he protected, and the kind of lifestyle he enjoyed. His wife, too, enjoyed this lifestyle. We know this because the men of God had to drag Lot and his family from the city before it was destroyed.25 They didn't want to leave. In fact, the scriptures tell us that Lot's wife looked (or turned) back and immediately fell to her death; turning into a pillar of salt.26

As if the story couldn't get any worse, after Lot and his two daughters made it out of the burning cities, his daughters conspired to get pregnant by their father. They wanted to preserve the family name since they had no brothers and their mother was now dead. 27

You may be thinking, like me, who would devise such a wicked plan, to actually get pregnant by their father? It beats me... but, I do know that if you hang around with evil long enough, you will become like it. Monkey see, monkey do!

Perhaps, the daughter's decision to commit such abominable acts was the result of the lifestyle they were accustomed to living. Who knows what all they witnessed in Sodom... or even in their own home. I've heard it said before that "sin will take you farther than you want to go, keep you longer than you want to stay and cost you more than you are willing to pay." That's why we have to be careful who and what we allow to influence our kids and what they are exposed to.

Because Lot and his wife tolerated and, perhaps, even enjoyed this kind of lifestyle, they perpetuated and instilled into their children a lifestyle unpleasing to God. Their choices brought about a generational curse in the bloodline. The eldest daughter gave birth to a son, Moab, who became the father of the Moabites. The youngest daughter gave birth to Ben-Ammi who became the father of the Amorites.[28] Both the Moabites and the Amorites were two of Israel's greatest enemies.

We are the gatekeepers of our homes... the thermostats. We set the tone of the atmosphere. What we allow and engage in, our children will partake of too. We must be wise and strategic like the Gazelle when it comes to raising our kids. When we operate outside of God's statutes and commandments, we set ourselves, our children and our future generations up to fail.

Monkey see, monkey do.

lebekah, Isaac & Sons

Genesis 27 captures another drama-filled episode of failed parenting. This time, a mother goes to great lengths to ensure her "favorite" son receives the blessing of his father. The story follows the life of Abraham & Sarah's son, Isaac and his family. This is the son whom Sarah actually birthed at the age of NINETY.

Isaac married a woman named Rebekah and they had twin boys, Esau and Jacob. Jacob was the younger son and Rebekah's favorite- a mama's boy, lol. Esau, the eldest son, was a hunter and a good cook. He was presumably Issacs's favorite as he was a man's man possessing all the qualities one would want in a son, especially his firstborn.

When Isaac was old and near death, he was preparing to bless his eldest son, Esau, for it was the custom in Antiquity that the oldest son received the birthright blessing from their father. If you recall the story of Abraham and how the Lord blessed him in Genesis 22, it is that same blessing that Isaac is now passing down to his oldest son, Esau, or so he thought.

Rebekah, Isaac's wife, overheard Isaac speaking with Esau about the blessing. She devised a plan and coerced Jacob, her favorite son, to deceive his father by pretending to be the older brother. This way he could steal his brother's birthright.

Her plan emerged and Jacob received the blessing instead of Esau. Esau was enraged by this, as you can probably imagine. He plotted to kill his baby brother, Jacob.

Rebekah's plan perpetuated in Jacob, a lifestyle of lies and deceit.

As parents, we do have our favorites and we really have no control over that. We favor who we favor and for various reasons. The problem for Rebekah was that she went too far. She didn't consider Esau's feelings in the matter nor the impact her decision would have on her children. It would be many, many years before Esau and Jacob would meet to reconcile. We have to be cognizant of our decisions as parents. We don't hurt (injure) a child because they aren't our favorite.

The love we have for the "favorite" child should never cast doubt on the love we have for all of our children. All children need love and acceptance regardless of who they are or what they've done because "love will cover a multitude of sin."29 The unconditional love of a parent has the power to positively influence the trajectory of a child's life forever.

In the end, Rebekah didn't even have to manipulate and sow discord in her family. You see, when she was pregnant with the twins, God promised her that "the older (son) would serve the younger son," meaning, Jacob would receive the blessing, instead of Esau.30 Rebekah didn't have to intervene or force it because God had already said it would happen. God would have brought it to pass.

Jochebed

The story of Moses' birth, found in Exodus 2:1-10, gives a very accurate account of the depths of a mother's love and just how far a mother will go to save her child. Filled with love, pain and redemption, these few verses speak to the essence of God's Grace and Mercy and how in even unfavorable situations, God's Plan and Purpose prevail.

In Exodus 1:22, the Pharaoh of Egypt issued a decree that all male Hebrew babies be thrown into the Nile River. The king wanted to cut off the Hebrew's ability to reproduce and to stunt their economic growth for they had become quite successful in Egypt. Under this new regime, annihilation of all newly born Hebrew boys ensued.

When Jochebed, Moses' mother, heard about the decree, she contrived a plan to hide Moses. "But, when she could hide him no longer, she got a papyrus basket for him and coated it with tar and pitch. Then she placed the child in it and put it among the reeds along the bank of the Nile."[31]

What I love most about this story is that Jochebed recognized that she could no longer care for her son, Moses, and that she needed to trust his care to someone else, more specifically, God. She had to trust the God of her faith to care for her infant child.

Jochebed placed Moses in the Nile hoping that he would land somewhere safe. She didn't just place him in any old basket either, but one craftly designed to maintain durability against the tide, and the threat of crocodiles and other sea creatures.

After Jochebed sent Moses down the Nile River, Pharaoh's daughter found him and wanted to keep him. Since he was an infant he needed to be nursed. Moses' sister (who kept watched over Moses' landing) went to Pharaoh's daughter and suggested that a Hebrew woman nurse the baby boy. Pharaoh's daughter obliged, and Moses' sister took him back to his mother Jochebed to be nursed (Exodus 2:4-9)!

Moses' birth mother was able to care for her son a little while longer until he was weened. Then she returned him to Pharaoh's daughter (Exodus 2:10). Moses went on to be raised in the kingdom safe and sound because of the courage and faith of his mother.

Sometimes, parents have to make a difficult decision to give their child up, either for adoption or to be raised by a more competent person, momentarily. There's a negative stigma in our society that says if women (and men) choose to allow someone else to raise their kids, that they are negligent. It's true that we have to take specific measures to protect ourselves from having unwanted children, like birth control or abstinence. But there are times when life happens, and parents are unable to care for their kids, whether temporarily or permanently. Making the hard decision to let someone else raise a child is a courageous act that expresses genuine love and concern for the child.

If you have had to make that hard decision, know that God loves you and is not mad at you. God still has an awesome plan for your life and that of your children. We never know how God is going to use you or the child. We don't always know how things will work out. But, let me tell you, Moses went on to live well and to become great. In fact, he returned to his people, led them out of bondage, and he is still revered by the Jews as Israel's greatest prophet!

David & Bathsheba

In 2 Samuel 11, we find the treacherous story of David and Bathsheba. David was the most powerful and greatest king ever noted in the Old Testament. He ruled over both Israel and Judah and was coined, "A man after God's own heart."[32] This meant that in all of David's doings, he inquired of the Lord. David loved the people of God and sought to do the will of God in all things.

David, however, was far from perfect. One day while walking on the roof of his palace, he spotted a gorgeous woman, Bathsheba, ironically, bathing. Get it... BATHsheba?! LOL. Well, David calls for her to come and sleep with him, although she was a married woman. Bathsheba's husband, Uriah, was gone fighting a war in David's army at the time of this encounter. She sleeps with David and ends up pregnant by him.

David sends for Uriah to come home hoping he'd have sex with Bathsheba in order to justify her pregnancy. 2 Samuel 11:6-12 says that Uriah returned from battle, but did not go home to Bathsheba. So, David sent word to have him placed on the front line, ensuring he'd be killed in battle. Scandalous, right?! I know!

David, in reality, took advantage of Bathsheba by exerting his power and authority as king. Having her husband killed nailed the coffin, figuratively and literally. God dealt with David by taking the life of the baby.[33]

The residual effects of David's sin show up in the following chapter of 2 Samuel 13. In this chapter, David's eldest son, Amnon, raped his half-sister, Tamar, because he was "madly in love with her."34 Then, Tamar's brother Absalom (David's son) turns around and kills Amnon. It's funny how "the sins of the father visit the sons."35 David's abuse of Bathsheba and the murder of Uriah came back to haunt him.

In the end, David and Bathsheba's situation turned around for good. They got married and had another son, Solomon, who became king after David. Solomon was highly favored of God and considered the 'wisest man ever known.'36

Know that God can turn your failures into favor! He can turn your guilt into grace but you have to be open and willing to always seek the Lord, whether up or down... in or out... good or bad. If you will just invite the Lord into every situation that you encounter, you'll see Him in every one of those situations. Your life will change for the better.

Hosea & Gomer

The story of Hosea and Gomer is one of immense fascination and intrigue as God tells a prophet, Hosea, to marry a prostituting and adulteress, Gomer. God commanded Hosea to marry Gomer as symbolic of His relationship to Israel. God is eternally faithful to Israel (His chosen people) and two-timing Israel is always unfaithful and rebellious to God.

The story goes that Hosea marries Gomer and they have a son. Shortly after, Gomer becomes pregnant not once, but twice, by other men.37 Hosea declares he will never "show love to her children, because they are the children of adultery," 38 but he names them according to the command of the Lord. Gomer's daughter, he named, Lo-

Ruhamah, meaning 'no mercy shown,' and her son, Lo-Ammi meaning 'you are not my people, I am not your God.'39

Gomer returned to prostitution and Hosea wanted to divorce her, but God began talking with him about His plan to restore Gomer; also symbolic of Him restoring Israel. 40 God instructs Hosea to redeem Gomer. That is, to buy her back from her pimps... or "lovers" as the Bible calls them. LOL. Hosea follows the command of the Lord and redeems his wife.41 Gomer agreed to go back with Hosea and to remain faithful to him just like Israel promised (time and time again) to return and to be faithful to God.

Hosea and Gomer's story contains several interesting dynamics, but we will focus on the children. We can discern if we are listening, the silent, deafening cries of Gomer's children, conceived through adulterous affairs. One could imagine Gomer's children being bitter and confused feeling unwanted and unloved.

Children conceived through adultery or rape often struggle with feelings of low self-worth. They spend a great deal of time searching for identity, acceptance and love, even to their detriment, sometimes. Marcus Garvey said, "A people without the knowledge of their past history, origin and culture is like a tree without roots."42 It's difficult to flourish without a solid foundation and understanding of who you are. It's even more challenging for children to respond appropriately under such adverse circumstances.

Both children and parents alike need to know that we are all indeed welcomed into the family of Believers and can be called 'children of the Most High God.' God will always accept you for His Word says in Psalm 27:10, "When your mother and father forsake you, I will take you in." God longs to give you a new identity, one rooted and grounded in Christ Jesus. Jesus knows all about this struggle for He, too, was named and raised by a man... not His biological Father.

Mary & Joseph

We can't talk about families of the Bible without referencing our Lord and Savior, Jesus Christ's family. Immaculately born of a virgin, Jesus was the eldest son of his mother, Mary, and step-father, Joseph. Scripture tells us in Matthew 1:18 that "After His mother Mary was betrothed to Joseph, before they came together (or had sexual intimacy), she was found with child of the Holy Spirit." Mary and Joseph had not yet consummated their relationship, nor had there been a marriage ceremony when Jesus was conceived.

In Jewish antiquity, there were three stages to marriage: (1) the engagement, usually arranged by the parents with a dowry paid to the bride's father, (2) the betrothal period which usually lasted about a year. During this time, the couple is considered husband and wife and in order to break the betrothal, a divorce has to occur and (3) the marriage ceremony[43] and consummation, through sexual intimacy.[44] Mary and Joseph were in the betrothal stage when Jesus was conceived.

Joseph wanted to divorce Mary when he found out she was pregnant. [45] You can imagine it being pretty hard to accept that she was pregnant by God, lol, but an angel of the Lord appeared to Joseph and reassured him of this

Truth.46 So Joseph married Mary and raised Jesus as his own son. Joseph raised the Son of God! My God!

You never know who or what your kids will become. Even if they're not your biological kids, you can still intervene and make a difference in their life. We need more men like Joseph who are willing to step up and raise kids who are not their own. We need men who love and protect kids, not leeches and predators, who only set out to hurt them.

Children are special and a priority to God. He says, "See that you do not despise one of these little ones. For I tell you that in Heaven their angels always see the face of my Father who is in Heaven."47 God is depending on you to raise children who become who He has created them to be. He has entrusted their care to you. You need to know that that's a high calling and you are more than able to fulfil the call.

Chapter 2: *The Call to Parent*

"Children are a heritage from the Lord, the fruit of the womb is a reward."[1]

Sometimes, I sit in amazement that God has entrusted me with such a precious gift in my son, Jai. Daily, his presence gives me spunk and a willingness to pursue life with excitement and great expectation for our future. I look forward to seeing all the many things he will accomplish in life and all the many ways God will use him.

You see, Jai is already performing significantly better than I was at his age. He's a homebody and easy going. I loved to run the street, so to speak, and was quite rebellious. He's intelligent and when he really applies himself, makes above average grades. I struggled somewhat academically and didn't put forth much effort at all. He has the favor of God on his life (as did I) and has a really bright future ahead of him.

I could go on and on about my son, speaking of all his accolades, but without the enabling, equipping and empowerment of the Holy Spirit, I would have nothing to brag about. For "unless the Lord builds the house, they that labor do so in vain."2 If it had not been for the Lord on our side, I don't know where we would be.

The Lord has made all the difference in our lives. It is the calling that He has placed on our lives that has enabled me to effectively parent (for the most part) as a single mother, and it is the Lord who has enable Jai to pursue all the wonderful things that God has for him. "It is the Lord's doing and it is marvelous in our sight."3

God has a plan and a purpose for gifting us with children. He didn't bless us with kids because we like them or did a good job at playing house when we were children. LOL. No, he has a purpose and that is to glorify Him. It's our job, as parents, to help our kids discover their purpose and to catapult them into the awesome destiny God has for them.

When I was a senior in high school my mother sat me down to watch a documentary called *I am a Promise: The Children of Stanton Elementary School*.4 It portrayed the lives of several inner-city youth in Philadelphia, PA. The children who attended Stanton Elementary School came from high poverty, crime-stricken communities. Several of the elementary aged kids had to care for themselves and their younger siblings as their parents were addicted to crack cocaine and other narcotics. The images of disparity and the immensely disheartening stories shared in the documentary still haunt me, today.

After watching the film my mother shared with me her desire for me to become a teacher, as she is an educator, herself. She told me she believed teaching was my calling and that I would fare well doing so in the inner-city. Boy was she right! Working with inner city youth has been my passion for over twenty years now. I have a keen interest in educating and empowering the marginalized, oppressed and disadvantaged.

I know it was the leading of the Holy Spirit that prompted my mother to speak to me that day about becoming a teacher. That was God's plan and purpose for creating me. I'm sure that if my mother and I never had that conversation, I would have still become a teacher... for God's Will will be accomplished in the earth. He would have gotten me where I needed to be. But, my mother's obedience to the leading of the Holy Spirit gave me direction and a sure foundation. I didn't have to search far and wide, being swayed by every idea of the enemy. No, I was clear that teaching was the way in which I needed to go and as a result of my obedience, have found much success living out my calling.

Another great illustration of how a mother (or any parent) can greatly influence their child's destiny is found in John 2:1-5. It reads, "on the third day a wedding took place at Cana in Galilee. Jesus' mother was there, and Jesus and his disciples had also been invited to the wedding. When the wine was gone, Jesus' mother said to Him, "They have no more wine." "Woman, why do you involve me?" Jesus replied. "My hour has not yet come." Jesus' mother said to the servants, "Do whatever He tells you." In other words, "Jesus, Your time has come and yes You are going to do what I say (my paraphrase)."

John 2:1-5 is often referred to as Jesus' First Miracle-when He turned water into wine. Jesus didn't know that the time had come for Him to showcase to the world His true identity. But, Mama knows best! Mary understood Who Jesus was and His potential. She understood purpose and recognized, like my mother, the season and timing in which best to act.

Mary's wisdom, coupled with Jesus' obedience to His mother, catapulted Him into His highest purpose and the most monumental season of His life. From that day forward, He became known as the *Chrîstos*, that is the Christ.[5]

God has given us the ability to see in our children what they can't always see in themselves. He's anointed us to raise them in the fear and admonition of God. God has given to us everything that we need to raise our children well. We are called to this!

Some might ask, *what is the call to parent?* It's an anointing given by God to all parents and caregivers enabling them to raise happy, healthy children in the fear and admonition of God (or as I often say, "who love God"). It is a call to partner with God to ensure our children reach their highest potential and greatest purpose in life. Raising kids in the "fear and admonition of God" is to raise kids who have a healthy self-awareness and identity of who they are in Christ Jesus.

The Call as Enabling

The call, *itself,* is the power or anointing that *enables* us to fulfil the calling. God is the enabler and does the enabling. He enables us to fulfill the call to parent. Because God called us to parent, evident by the fact that we have children, He has also given us the power to effectively parent the children He's given. For God would NEVER call us to do something that we can't do. We can be confident that we can raise happy, healthy kids in the fear and admonition of the Lord because of His enabling.

God's enabling is not predicated on submission to His Lordship. By His Goodness, He enables us all, whether we accept Him as Lord and Savior or not. We don't have to submit to God in order to parent. But, oh how much sweeter are the days when we do accept Him as our Lord and Savior.

If we are to raise happy, healthy kids who love God, however, we *must* enter into agreement (a partnership) with God through submission to His Will for our lives. It is only by submitting to His Will, through obedience to His Word, that we can enjoy the abundant life He's promised us. Thankfully, He enables us to do that, too!

I remember the day I came into partnership with the Lord to parent my son, Jai. It was in September, 2003. My ex-husband had just announced that he wanted a divorce and I was devastated. I remember laying on the couch in our living room, crying and feeling mighty bad about myself, lol, when I heard the peaceful voice of the Lord say, "just Trust Me!" I was so broken at the time because of my failed marriage and a slew of other painful events of my past. I said to God, 'I don't even trust my own mother!" It's not as if my mother had done anything wrong, but rather that I was mad at the world. I trusted no one. Saying that I didn't even trust my mother, showed the extent of my pain and mistrust.

I had hit rock bottom and felt that no one could help me back up again. But, nevertheless, I said, 'Ok God. I'll trust You but it won't be easy." It has not always been easy, but I believe my "yes" to God that day enabled the many blessings, love and support that I have consistently receive from the Lord.

The Call as Equipping

The call to parent is equipping. God equips us with everything we need to effectively parent happy, healthy kids who love Him. The tools God gives are spiritual, financial, physical and emotional. They consist of employment, intuition, an unexpected blessing, a word of instruction/discipline, or even a mentor or coach who takes special interest in our children. Whatever the need, God supplies. For He is concerned with every detail of our lives. Everything that concerns us, concerns God.

Here's a funny story... I remember a time when I was sure that there was a mouse, or some other rodent in my house. I sensed something breathing and living around me. LOL. Normally, I would demand that my son kill whatever intrusively trespassed into our home (like a spider or some other insect) and he'd usually come to my rescue. But, he was in New York with his father for the Summer. So, I was on my own.

I remember praying and asked the Lord to help me kill this mouse or whatever it was. I begged him to send a man or someone that could catch this rodent for me. LOL. "Send anyone, God," I said.

The next day, I came home from work and had to use the restroom. While in the restroom, I could hear something rattling in the trashcan in the kitchen. I sprinted to the kitchen, as you can imagine, grabbed the trash bag and darted out the house to throw the rodent into the trashcan outside, pushed the can to the street and ran back in the house as fast as I could. LOL. I didn't dare look in the bag to see what it was, but I'm confident that it was the rodent! The Lord had caught the mouse (or whatever it was) and threw it in the trash for me!! LOL.

God really is concerned about everything that concerns us. He will show up time and time again and will equip us with what we need, when we trust Him. I really appreciate the many ways God comes through for this single, sometimes scary, mother.

Once we understand the *power in the call* to parent, we become more empowered to engage ourselves in partnership with God. Parenting becomes more of an honor and less of a burden when we understand that God is with us. We become better people... better parents, as a result of our partnership with God.

When we know that God is with us, we can trust that He will take care of us. We can rest assured knowing that all will be well with us. When we know that God is with us, we are less afraid to handle the challenges that all parents experience when raising little people who grow up. When we know that God is with us, we can expect every situation to work out for our good.[6]

God empowers us to embrace the call to parent. Embracing the call is our response to God's assured partnership with us forever. Knowing that God is always with us gives us confidence to believe that everything will be alright.

The Calling of God

God has always called both men and women alike to accomplish His purpose in the earth. Whether that is to deliver His people from bondage or birthing the Messiah, God has chosen to use people to accomplish His purpose in the Earth. The Bible provides many examples of what a calling looks like and the power it possesses. We see what embracing a call can accomplish through the lives of those who previously answered the call of God on their lives. These men and women have shown us what it takes to be faithful to the call of God and the rewarding outcome we can expect when we partner with God.

Samuel

The story of the Prophet Samuel begins in 1 Samuel 1-3. Hannah, who would later birth Samuel was barren and could not conceive a child. Her husband Elkanah, had another wife who was fruitful and multiplying, lol, her name was Peninnah. The Word tells us Elkanah loved Hannah the most, however, and that ensued a hating-Peninnah to taunt Hannah because of her barrenness.[7]

One day, Hannah, while praying, made a vow to the Lord. She promised God that if He would bless her with a son that she in return would give him back to the Lord.[8] The Lord was merciful to Hannah and gave her a son, Samuel.

Hannah fulfilled her vow to God. When the child was weaned, she took him to the high priest, Eli, to be raised by him and to serve in the temple of the Lord all the days of his life, as she promised.

One night, when Samuel was about 11 years old, the Lord *called* him. Samuel ran to Eli and said, "Here I am; you called me." God's voice must have sounded, to Samuel, like his surrogate father Eli. But Eli said, "I did not call; go back and lie down." So, Samuel went and laid back down. Again, the Lord called, Samuel. Samuel got up and went to Eli and said, "Here I am; you called me." "My son," Eli said, "I did not call; go back and lie down."9

This "calling" was repeated again at which time Eli realized that it was the Lord calling Samuel. He told Samuel "Go and lie down, and if He calls you, say, 'Speak, Lord, for your servant is listening." So, Samuel went back to bed. The Lord came and stood there, calling as at the other times, "Samuel! Samuel!" Then Samuel said, "Speak, for your servant is listening."10

This marked the beginning of Samuel's powerful ministry as Prophet to the people of God. In fact, he is still revered as one of Israel's greatest prophets. He shared the Word of the Lord with God's people, pronounced the judgements of God and he called nations to repent.11 Everything he spoke concerning the Lord deemed to be true.

God created, called and anointed Samuel to be a Prophet to the nations. Samuel fulfilled his call and served God all the days of his life. He served so well, in fact, when he died all of Israel attended his funeral and "mourned for him."[12]

David

In 1 Samuel 16, Samuel the prophet, was given an assignment by God to anoint David as king. Israel already had a king at the time, Saul, whom the people chose.[13] However Saul did evil in the eyes of the Lord,[14] so God ordered Samuel to anoint David (whom God had chosen) as king of Israel.

God told Samuel to go to Bethlehem to anoint one of Jesse' sons but He didn't tell him which son it would be. Jesse brought before Samuel seven sons whom both Jesse and Samuel knew would surely be chosen by God to be king because of their appearance and stature. But God told Samuel, "Do not consider his appearance or his height because I have rejected him (them)."[15]

After seeing all of Jesse's boys and none of them being the king whom God was calling, Samuel asked Jesse if he had another son. Jesse responded, "well, there is still the youngest, but he is tending the sheep."[16] Samuel had Jesse to send for the young boy. Turns out he was God's chosen vessel! Samuel anointed David and he became king instead of Saul.

Many theologians suggest that Jesse may not have been David's real father, but rather David was a product of his mother's infidelity. That might explain why Jesse was hesitant about bringing David before Samuel when Samuel asked to see all of Jesse's sons. The good news is that none of that really matters, though, in the scope of things. God will call and use anyone God chooses to complete the purpose of God in the world!

David was a loner and very courageous. When Samuel found and anointed him, David was tending the flock, for he was a shepherd. He was known for putting his own life in danger for the sake of his flock and the people of Israel, even before becoming king. He loved God and the people of God and it's no wonder why God coined him, "a man after His own heart."[17]

Mary, the Mother of Jesus

Mary, the mother of Jesus, was pledged to be married to Joseph when she received her call.[18] The Angel Gabrielle appeared to the virgin Mary and told her that she was favored of God to birth the Savior of the world, God's Only Begotten Son. God called Mary to be His Baby Mama, if you will, LOL.

She made some serious life-altering decisions in that moment. I can only imagine the fear she was experiencing and the many questions of doubt swarming her head. Would she lose the man she loved? Could she handle single parenting in such a theocratic society? How would she handle the shame and ostracism that would come as a result of her decision? Mary chose to heed the call to parent, even the possibility of single parenting. She chose to accept whatever she encountered with faith in God. Her response was simply, "I am the Lord's servant. May everything you have said about me come true."[19]Mary was a bad chick! She was courageous and willing to put it all on the line as a result of her faith in God.

Rané Monique, M.Div.

In parenting, especially single parenting, you may have to put it all on the line to do what God has called you to do. You won't always know *who or when* someone will come alongside to help you raise your children. But, you can rest assured that God will be with you, just as close as He was to Mary. You can rest assured that everything He has said about you will come true for God is faithful. He will do just what He says!

The Disciples

Perhaps, you already know the story of Jesus' calling of His twelve Disciples and how they chose to leave the life they were living to follow Him. Special recognition is given to these men because there were others whom Jesus called that chose not to follow Him. For the ones who did, however, they would go on to see and do great and mighty things for the Lord.

We see a powerful illustration of this in Matthew 10. We are told, "**He (Jesus) called** His twelve disciples to Him **and gave them authority** to drive out evil spirits and to heal every disease and sickness."[20] Notice here that Jesus didn't just call His Disciples, but He gave them purpose *and* equipped them for their mission.

All of Jesus' disciples were unique and they all utilized their gifts according to their purpose. Andrew, Peter, James and John were all fishermen. Matthew, otherwise known as Levi was a tax collector. Simon was a Zealot, or political activist/revolutionary, and Judas was a treasurer.[21] The scriptures do not reveal the occupation of the other disciples-Bartholomew, James, Phillip, Thaddeus and Thomas.

There's a powerful lesson to be gleaned from the calling of these twelve disciples: Numbers, demographics, upbringing, etc. are not prerequisites for the call of God. The call transcends race, class and ethnicities. God can use and has need of us all.

Jesus' ministry only lasted three years AND He only had twelve folks helping him! But He was committed to His calling. Many people were healed, delivered and at most, the whole world now has access to eternal life through the ministry and leadership of Jesus Christ and His disciples.

My Calling

May 15, 2004, I was living in Greensboro, North Carolina, had just separated from my ex-husband and was determined to develop a deeper relationship with Jesus Christ. My church at the time, Evangel Fellowship Church of God in Christ, offered the School of Prayer on Saturday mornings.

This particular Saturday we were studying *Praying in the Spirit* and were all on cloud nine. The prophetic was poured out in abundance and I received confirmation of things I'd prayed for the night before regarding my gifts and calling.

When I left church and got in my car the Lord began to speak to me. I was in utter amazement that I was hearing the audible voice of God. I mean, I was freaking out! God told me about my calling and explained to me why some things had occurred in my life as they had.

I was so overwhelmed with emotion that I said, "stop, I can't take this." And, God stopped talking to me... Then I was like, "No! Come back" LOL, for it was the greatest moment of my life. It was the greatest peace I'd ever experienced. But, God had finished speaking. It was that day that I desired to be in the presence of the Lord every opportunity that I got.

People ask me what the Voice of the Lord sounds like. His voice encompasses all of Who God is. It is Peaceful, yet Strong. Comforting, yet Frightening. It is freakishly amazing and there's no question of Who is speaking. You just know it's God.

It was so comforting for God to show me that my life has meaning and that the things I had experienced were not in vain. I approached life with a new perspective and outlook that day. I had a greater understanding and belief of Who God Is. I could see that a new day was dawning in my life and that I could begin burying the pain of my past. I was reassured that God had not forgotten about me, nor had He given up on me. I knew that God was present and that He was doing something in my life, even if I didn't quite understand what He was doing.

God has a purpose and a plan for everything that He does and everyone that He calls. When He formed you in your mother's womb, He had a plan for your life. He had a plan for your parent's life. He has a plan for your children. God is the "same yesterday, today and forevermore."[22] He's Faithful and His purpose for us is always "good and not evil, to give us hope and a future."[23] We just have to trust Him.

Chapter 3: *Generational Blessings*

"For I, the Lord your God, am a jealous God, visiting the iniquity of the fathers upon the children to the third and fourth generations of those who hate Me, but showing mercy to thousands, to those who love Me and keep My commandments."

Deuteronomy 5:9-10

I once had a woman prophesy to me that I had blessings all around me. I had a hard time receiving her prophecy because of who I saw when I looked in the mirror. All I saw was the B.C. Rané. That is, "before Christ," lol. I saw the not smart enough, not cute enough, not good enough version of myself. But, the more I walked with Christ, the better I understood what she meant. The more you walk in obedience to God's Word, the more blessings will overtake you.

A popular cliché used by church people in response to someone asking how they are doing, is to say, "I'm blessed and highly favored." I often tell people that we confuse the goodness of God with the blessings of God. Everyone who says they're blessed and highly favored, may in reality be experiencing the goodness of the Lord. You see, God is good to everyone. He provides for us all. He makes a way out of no way. He loves us all. God is always showing His goodness and mercy to all of humanity whether we love Him or not... whether we acknowledge His goodness or not. God is always good to us all!

It's one thing to experience the goodness of God in your life, but it's a far greater thing to have the blessings of the Lord on your life and the lives of your children. We desire the latter but don't always acquire it, for it is only obtained through obedience to God's Word and faith in Jesus Christ.

When God appeared to Abraham in Genesis 22, He told him, "I swear by Myself, declares the Lord... I will surely bless you and make your descendants as numerous as the stars in the sky and as the sand on the seashore. Your descendants will take possession of the cities of their enemies and through your offspring all nations on earth will be blessed, because you have obeyed me." This promise to bless Abraham and his offspring is referred to as the Abrahamic Covenant.

A covenant is an agreement between two parties. It usually involves a comparable, lateral exchange. I may agree to tutor your child for a certain number of weeks in exchange for you providing lawncare services for me. This is a comparable, lateral exchange because the terms of the agreement require us both to put in work and to make sacrifices.

God's covenant with Abraham, however, was not a comparable, lateral exchange. God promised to always bless Abraham and his children so long as Abraham obeyed the command of the Lord. What a blessing! Obviously, God is in a higher place of authority than Abraham and God is the One providing the blessing. God gave Abraham everything in exchange for Abraham trusting that God could do it. That's an astounding deal if you ask me.

In the Bible, God is often seen making covenant agreements with humanity. He made a few with Abraham. He made covenants with Noah, a prostitute named Rahab, and King David, to name a few people. [1]

When you enter into covenant with God, God will always keep His Word. He will fulfill the promises of the covenant. Hebrews 6:13 states, "when God made His promise to Abraham, since there was no one greater for Him to swear by, He swore by Himself." I love that! How many times have people promised us things and never delivered on those promises?! Too many to count. But, God is not like man. Hallelujah!

When God makes a promise to us, He always makes good on it. You can bet your bottom dollar that what He says, will come to pass. God has never made a promise that He didn't keep. It may take some time for the promise to manifest, so we have to learn to wait on Him, but it will happen. Hebrews 6:15 lets us know that "after waiting patiently, Abraham received what was promised."

rational Curses and Blessings

ronomy 5:9-10 says, "For I, the Lord your God, *am* a jealous God, visiting the iniquity of the fathers upon the children to the third and fourth *generations* of those who hate Me, but showing mercy to thousands, to those who love Me and keep My commandments."

In every family there are curses and blessings that follow the bloodline, otherwise known as generational curses and generational blessings. A generational curse is a destructive pattern that repeatedly exists in a family. In the same way that everyone in the family has a distinct facial feature, such as their nose, lips, eyes and even hair, a generational curse is a negative behavior that is common amongst many family members.

Any destructive pattern that presents itself over and over again affecting multiple people in the same family, is more than likely a generational curse. For example, you may find that in one family many people struggle with drug or alcohol addictions. Grandma was an alcoholic; her children are alcoholics. Aunts and uncles all have struggles with addiction. Cousins and grandchildren have drug and alcohol addiction. That's a generational curse.

Generational curses present themselves in various forms. A friend of mine acknowledged a generational curse on her family that has prevented the women from getting and/or staying married. She described the women in her family as being very strong, take-charge women and unwilling to put up with much "foolishness from a man." She has divorced three times, her mother has never been married and all her sisters, aunts and female cousins have either divorced or have never been married, although they all have children. As a result, they have all raised their children in fatherless homes and for many of them, in poverty.

Having a family history of incarceration is another generational curse. This is where just about every male (or even female) in the family has spent time in jail or the penal system. There are all kinds of generational curses. A history of teenage, unwed pregnancies or abortions usually stem from a generational curse. If someone is being raised without their mother or father and it just so happens that their mother or father, cousins, aunts and uncles were raised without theirs, too, it is a generational curse. Maybe no one in the family has graduated from high school or college and poverty runs rampant in the family. That's a generational curse. Basically, any destructive behavior that becomes a pattern in one's family, is a curse.

Generational curses are learned behaviors and patterns. They are the result of unresolved, unchecked, undisciplined behaviors that run rampant continue to negatively impact families. Because they are learned behaviors, they can be unlearned and dispelled. When we overcome addiction or another generational curse... when we draw the line in the sand and say "no more... when we refuse to allow toxic people and situations into our lives and our children's lives, curses can be broken.

All curses are evil and are not of God. They are of the devil and his regime. They do not have to exist or persist any longer in the lives of the children of God. We can forge a new path, one built on righteousness and truth. Generational curses are built on deception and lies. Someone, somewhere believed a lie of the enemy... "this drug won't hurt you," "that man would never hurt your child," "You're not smart enough to go to college because no one else in your family did." They are lies of the enemy... the enemy of your soul.

The purpose and design of the enemy is to entangle you in destructive mindsets and behaviors hindering your ability to become all that God has purposed for you to become. So, we have to change our way of thinking. We must get free from the entanglements of our past and generational curses, in order to raise happy, healthy kids who love God. Because broken parents produce even more severely broken children. However, when we receive Jesus Christ as Lord and Savior we have power and authority to break the curse off of our lives and our children for generations to come. Curses persist when we are unaware of who we are, our power and authority, and the right we've been given as a result of our belief in Jesus Christ.

Blessings In HIM

In the Old Testament, God gave the Israelites a specific set of rules and guidelines they were to follow in order to please God and to live as children of God. These commandments, procedures and guidelines became known as The Law. When Israel followed God's commands, they experienced blessings and great success. Deuteronomy 28 depicts this blessing:

"If you fully obey the Lord your God and carefully follow all his commands I give you today, the Lord your God will set you high above all the nations on earth. All these blessings will come on you and accompany you if you obey the Lord your God: You will be blessed in the city and blessed in the country. The fruit of your womb will be blessed, and the crops of your land and the young of your livestock—the calves of your herds and the lambs of your flocks. Your basket and your kneading trough will be blessed. You will be blessed when you come in and blessed when you go out. The Lord will grant that the enemies who rise up against you will be defeated before you. They will come at you from one direction but flee from you in seven. The Lord will send a blessing on your barns and on everything you put your hand to. The Lord your God will bless you in the land he is giving you.

The Lord will establish you as his holy people, as he promised you on oath, if you keep the commands of the Lord your God and walk in obedience to him. Then all the peoples on earth will see that you are called by the name of the Lord, and they will fear you. The Lord will grant you abundant prosperity—in the fruit of your womb, the young of your livestock and the crops of your ground—in the land he swore to your ancestors to give you.

The Lord will open the heavens, the storehouse of his bounty, to send rain on your land in season and to bless all the work of your hands. You will lend to many nations but will borrow from none. The Lord will make you the head, not the tail. If you pay attention to the commands of the Lord your God that I give you this day and carefully follow them, you will always be at the top, never at the bottom. Do not turn aside from any of the commands I give you today, to the right or to the left, following other gods and serving them."

When Israel was faithful to God by observing the Law and keeping God's commandments, they were blessed. But, when they were disobedient and didn't keep the commands of the Lord, they were cursed. The curse contradicted the blessing and the consequence of disobedience brought doom, gloom, unfruitfulness and ultimately death. 2

In Antiquity, when someone sinned, the Law outlined specific penalties for that sin. For example, "If any member of the community sins unintentionally and does what is forbidden in any of the Lord's commands, when they realize their guilt and the sin they have committed becomes known, they must bring as their offering for the sin they committed a female goat without defect."3 An animal had to be sacrificed because "without the shedding of blood, there is no remission of sin (or forgiveness).4

The priests would sacrifice the goat according to the instructions of the Law. Then, the Lord would accept their

offering as a form of atonement between that persc
God. They were forgiven and set free from the pen
that sin. *the tabernacle, or place of worship
which was the high st*

In Once a year, the high priest would go into the Holy of
Holies to offer a sacrifice for all the people of Israel. When
the high priest poured the blood of the sacrifice on the Mercy
Seat, if God accepted the sacrifice, the people were forgiven
and would have great success in the new year. If God
rejected the sacrifice, the high priest would drop dead on
the spot and Israel would be cursed for a period of time.
This was to fulfill God's righteous judgement of the law.

When Jesus came, died on a cross and was
resurrected, He "redeemed us from the curse of the law,
having become a curse for us: for it is written, cursed is
every one that hangs on a tree (or cross)."[5] Jesus became
sin, paid the penalty of sin, and made it possible for us to
live blameless lives before God. He also approved us for the
blessing; all who believes in Him.

It is Jesus' shed blood on the cross that affords us
forgiveness of our sins, reconciliation to the Father AND
qualifies us for the blessing. Jesus, when crucified cried out,
"It is finished"[6] meaning that there was now total & complete
access to the Father with all rights, privileges and benefits
for all who believe in Him. He became the ultimate and final
sacrifice for the sins of the whole world! So, when we are "in
HIM," meaning that we accept Him as Lord and Savior and
are committed to following and obeying HIM, we have
abundant life and blessings. We have access to all of the
promises of God. Through our confession of faith in Jesus

Christ, all of them are ours! Further good news is that the blessing is not simply for us, but for our children's children, because God is faithful to His covenant (partnership) with us.

It's true that when we are born again, we are under a new covenant, a covenant of grace through our Lord and Savior Jesus Christ. But, grace is not an endorsement to sin. But, when we sin (or fall short), we can repent (turn away from sin) and get back up. We are not penalized, or condemned by God when we repent. That's the grace that we have in Christ Jesus. He's already paid the penalty for our sins. He said in Matthew 5:17 that He "did not come to abolish the law, but to fulfil it," meaning that God's Word still stands for He is "the same yesterday, today and forevermore." We are still to obey His Commandments. When we do, we are blessed and the Lord promises to bless our children, too.

wkbk, 33

The Bible is filled with so many wonderful promises concerning our children. When we partner with God to raise our kids, we have access to them all. Let's look at some of these great promises and the ramifications that it has on our parenting.

"Children are a blessing and a gift from the Lord."- Psalm 127:3₇

I met a woman of faith several years ago who just looked as if the blessing of the Lord was upon her, lol. She had five boys (was pregnant with her sixth son at the time of our meeting), all ranging in age from ten months to eighteen years old. All the boys had biblical names, were homeschooled until a certain age, honor students, ate healthy snacks, and very likeable kids. They were just people you know the Lord has blessed.

The woman joked a lot about why God would bless *kept* her with so many boys when she didn't even want kids as a *little girl.* Of course, everyone around her could obviously see that the reason the Lord kept blessing her with more and more children was because He could trust her to do a good job of raising them. That's not to say that all parents with a lot of children are doing a great job at parenting. Just like we can't assume that someone, like myself, who has *an* only one child is doing a poor job at parenting. The point is that this woman was obviously doing a great job with her children and the Lord continued to bless her.

The truth of the matter is that all children are a blessing from God and are not to be viewed as a curse. Children aren't hindrances but blessings God sends to enhance and enrich our lives and to make us better people. It may not always look like the blessing is on us or our children's lives, but we have to have faith and know that it is. We have to recondition our hearts and minds to believe the truth of God's Word concerning our children. "Children are a blessing and a gift from the Lord."[8]

"The blessing of the Lord makes rich and adds no sorrow."- Proverbs 10:22
If "children are a blessing, (and) the blessing makes rich and adds no sorrow," we should be enjoying our children every day, right? Why is that on *there are* some days, I *we* don't feel blessed and *our children* my child does not *above* reflect the blessing that God promised

If you're like me,

43

is on our lives? If, in fact, we are blessed, why have there been more days than I want to count, where I feel sorrowful? I feel defeated, sometimes. There are days when I simply don't feel blessed.

It is in those times that I have to remind myself of this scripture and that I may not always feel blessed, but I am indeed blessed. Our children's actions and behaviors don't always portray the blessing, but they are blessed, too. The blessing is not about a feeling, it's about our faith in God's Word. Who does God say that we are? He calls us blessed. If we predicated the essence of our being on our feelings, we'd all be a mess.

Jesus says in John 10:9-10, "the enemy comes to steal, kill and destroy, but I have come that you may have life and have it more abundantly." The devil works hard at ensuring we don't enjoy our lives or our children. He loves to steal our joy and often uses our children to do so.

There was a time when my son made a couple of really bad decisions and it placed a huge strain on our relationship. There was literally no joy in our home for about a month. I was stressed out about the "what-ifs and the how-could-hes," and he was stressed out from the serious amount of discipline (punishment) that he was receiving from his father and I. Satan was having a field day with us all.

He wanted us mad and confused, for he's the author of confusion. He wanted to keep us down and depressed so that we could not move on and continue to enjoy our lives.

We had to decide to forgive and move on. We decided to not let satan steal another moment of our peace or our joy.

There are so many things that come to steal our joy and destroy our peace, but we have a promise from God that we won't live sorrowful lives when we put our trust in Him. He promises to "keep in perfect peace, those whose mind is stayed on Him." God is always leading us toward restoration with one another and with Him. He's always attracting us to a life of peace and the absence of sorrow.

"Raise a child in the way that he should go and when he is older he won't depart from it."- Proverbs 22:6

This is probably one of the most difficult promises to believe God for, lol, because it requires much patience before you see the manifestation of the promise. The premise of the scripture, and if I can paraphrase, is that you have to remain faithful through the long-haul of raising your children without seeing instant results. There will be some sleepless nights, tears, anguish, unsettling, feelings of loneliness and despair. There will be some heartache before you actually see that your kids were listening to you after all. Sometimes, it will take a good, long while before you can say with total assurance, "you know what, they're going to be just fine."

Until that time comes, stay with it and declare it anyway, that they will be just fine, because it's true. They will be. When we raise our children in the way that they should go, that is, in the fear and admonition of the Lord, we will see the fruits of our labor because God has promised.

God promised that what we instill in our children will come back to their remembrance when they need it and when they are grown, they will still be walking in obedience to our parenting and God's Word. If you're struggling to see the light at the end of the tunnel with your child(ren), keep teaching, keep praying, keep disciplining, keep sacrificing and definitely keep trusting God. You will see the manifestation of your hard work and you'll be so amazed at what you and God have accomplished together!

In Seminary, there was a popular saying that "God can't make a peanut butter and jelly sandwich and give it to your neighbor." Now, of course God can, but, God chooses instead to partner with us to feed our neighbors. You and God are the majority. He'll provide, you do the work and you and your children will enjoy the harvest!

All your children shall be taught of the Lord and great shall be the peace of your children." – Isaiah 54:13
So much has been lost in today's society as we move further and further away from God. People lack a conscience; many children appear heartless and fewer and fewer people see the significance of going to church and fellowshipping with other Believers. There's been a great falling away from the faith.

Our children are being taught that anything goes, and that right is wrong and wrong is right. It's becoming harder for our children to know the difference between right and wrong. Our children are being coerced into living lives unpleasing to God in order to fit into a mold they were never created to join. It's becoming quite difficult for parents to raise their children in the fear and admonition of God because of the societal demand to comply. *Conform to with unrighteousness.*

With all the many pressures of life, we still have to instill in our children the truth of God's Word and persuade them to believe that they are who God says they are. In spite of the influences that they see on YouTube, Instagram and Snapchat, we still have the challenge of coaxing them to believe that who God says they are is who they really want to become. We can't let society dictate who our kids are, or who they will become. They are who God says they are and who we (God and I) are raising them to be.

Much of my *young* parenting has been trying to instill into my son who he is in Christ Jesus. He likes secular music, and some of it, I can tolerate. Others, not so much, LOL! Listening to some of the lyrics is *can be* depressing because they don't adequately reflect our life or his upbringing. He's never had to sell drugs to feed his family. He knows nothing about being on the street. He's never missed a meal and never been arrested. Other than peer pressure, his grades and his health, he really has no major concern, lol.

Much of the music that our kids listen to nowadays comes straight from the pits of Hell. It's designed to take our kids to a dark place. This is one reason why we see an influx of kids committing violent acts and suicide. Satan wants to destroy our children.[9]

Parents must remind our children *kids* that they are children of the Light. They need to know that anyone can put anything *yours* over a musical beat. Anyone can post whatever they want to social media. There *they* don't have to be people of integrity or truth when posting, just have a thought or idea. A social media post, a song or YouTube video should not be the standard for which our kids attain. Jesus is the standard based off of emotions and when we are led by our emotions, anything is bound to happen.

It's an arduous task to cultivate peace into the minds of our children, but simply being mindful of their influences, eases the load. It's impossible to totally shield them from worldly influences and probably not a good idea to even try. However, we can limit the negative interactions and instruct our children in the "way that they should go." When we do our part, God works on our behalf to accomplish what we can't. We have to teach them God's Word.

Children's children are a crown to the aged, and parents are the pride of their children.—Proverbs 17:6

I've heard it said before that the best day of a person's life is the day they have grandchildren. I've also heard, "you love your kids on one level, but the love you have for your grandchildren tips the scale." Parents and grandparents are always so proud of their kids. They'll boast all day about their grandchildren if you have the time to listen.

Rarely do they have anything negative to say about their grandkids. Parents, too, often admit that they are exceedingly proud of their children.

I wonder how many of you have ever considered your children's perception of you as their parent. Would they speak highly of you? Do they want you to meet their friends, or are they ashamed and embarrassed of you? Are you happy and productive most of the time? Do you exude joy and peace or are you bitter and angry all the time to anyone other than your friends and immediate circle? Can your children have friends over? Are you hospitable and kind, or mean and distant?

A friend of mine was having a difficult time communicating with her adult children. They were always clashing because of the expectations they had of one another. My friend was disappointed that her children didn't measure up to her standards and expectations that she had for their lives. Her children were angry because they felt like nothing they did ever measured up to her expectations, and they, too, felt like she wasn't meeting their needs as their mother. They all had unrealistic expectations for each other and when neither of them measured up to those standards, a conflict would ensue.

When my friend realized that she was not the only one who felt betrayed and let down, and when she acknowledged her children's pain, their relationship began to heal. They learned to give each other the grace to be human. They learned how to better communicate their expectations and needs with one another. They learned to listen from the heart and not from a place of bitterness. The scripture tells us that "in all thy getting, get an understanding."10 We want our kids to be just as proud of us as we are of them. This happens when we seek to understand each other, instead of demanding to be heard."11

"Repent and be baptized, every one of you in the name of Jesus Christ for the forgiveness of sins. And you will receive the gift of the Holy Spirit. The promise is for you and your children, and for all who are far off- for all whom the Lord our God will call."- Acts 2:38-39

This is a wonderful promise to us that regardless of what it looks like, God promises to save our children. The only prerequisite is that we have submitted our lives to Him. God has so many wonderful promises and so many awesome things in store for us when we trust Him.

When we lead lives pleasing unto God He promises that all will be well with our children. This doesn't mean that there will never be trouble or opposition. There will be. But, it means that God will always see us through. We are always helped. We are always rescued by our God.

We have promises from God. Promises of blessings & not curses, when we do His will. When we learn to trust Him & stand on His word, we'll see those promises of blessings come to pass in our lives.

Chapter 4: *Assessing Your Parenting Style*

"For which of you, intending to build a tower, does not sit down first and count the cost, whether he has enough to finish it?"

Luke 14:28, NKJV

About 34% of all households in America consist of single-parent and blended families.1 For various reasons, the family structure of times past, where both natural parents are represented in the home, rarely exists in society today. It's becoming more and more common to see children being raised by older siblings, grandparents and even distant family members including aunts, uncles, cousins and step-families.

No two families are alike, regardless of how we try to compare them. Every family has their own unique set of strengths, challenges and needs. Because of this, there is no one-size-fits-all blueprint on how to raise happy, healthy kids who love God. Parents must assess their own family dynamics to construct a viable winning plan conducive for their family.

In order to do that, we must first reflect upon *our* own parent's method of parenting and the family dynamics in which we were raised. Were parents present? Were they Engaged? Did they work all the time? Were they strict? Abusive? Critical? Mean? How was the relationship between other siblings? These and other familial questions are all very helpful to consider when formulating a winning plan for your family.

My Family

Growing up, I wanted a lot of kids because I sometimes felt like an only child. You see, my sister, Reecia, who is about five years older than I, went away to college in North Carolina when I was in middle school. My mother, too, began working nights during that time. So, I spent my teenage years at home with my father in the evenings after school.

My father has always loved and cared for our family above all else. He's a hard worker and provided well for us, growing up. He has a Type A Personality which means he strives for perfection in all that he does. He can be opinionated, stubborn and even critical at times, but he will do anything for his family and those he loves.

My mother is a gentle giant. She's smart and successful and is a fashion extraordinaire. She has been a submitted wife to my father for almost 50 years, of which I kind of resented growing up. I wanted her to be more outspoken, especially as it pertained to my father's personality and outspokenness. As I matured and married, I understood that she did speak up and checked my father when needed, lol, just not in front of my sister and I.

My sister and I both sometimes view our childhood through the lens of an only child since there was a bit of a gap in our ages. I was the nagging little sister and she was the never-wanted-to-be- bothered big sister. We clashed. We didn't share secrets or get advice from one another. We were very distant. However, when I was afraid at night, I could sleep with her. When she left for college, my friends and I would visit her for an always fun and eventful weekend. We may not have been close growing up, but we always had each other's back and as we grew older, our affection for one another grew stronger. Today, we are not only sisters, but the best of friends.

I think it's safe to say that my family was not as tight knit and unified as we are today. We weren't as spiritually sound. We weren't as content in our lives as we are now. We weren't as sensitive to each other's needs, back then.

Today, we work more at becoming the unified front that we need to be. We make it a priority to gather together weekly. Those gatherings consist of lots of laughs, intellectually stimulating conversations, music, food and plenty of petty shenanigans. We see God active in our lives and are learning what it means more and more each day to live the abundant life that God promised us.

Three Parenting Styles

Parenting is challenging. Seems kids won't act right and parents are at their wits end. Truth is, however, it's never a "bad-kid" or an "irresponsible-adult problem, altogether. Rather, it's a compilation of unrealistic and unmet expectations, miscommunication and misunderstandings, and not having a clear, honest vision and strategy for the family.

Parents must honestly assess their own parenting style in order to get the good results they desire for their kids. You have to be honest about where you are right now, for you can't change what you won't confront. You can raise the kind of kids you want to see, but it will take perseverance, patience and a whole lot of faith in God to do so. But, you can do it!

I've concluded that most parents display characteristics of three different parenting styles. They are ***reclusive, exclusive and inclusive*** parenting. Although varying in degree and structure (since no two families are alike), parents can usually identify with one. It's also possible to fall in between categories, as we are often transitioning from one stage to the next as we are empowered by God to do so.

Reclusive Parenting

Reclusive Parenting is parenting that refuses to confront any challenge or disappointment that presents itself. This type of parent turns a blind eye to issues. They may tell themselves that all is well when in fact, they know that it's not. They're uninterested in the truth but only in what feels good to them and what they are comfortable with handling. In reclusive parenting, family problems are never dealt with and things are often swept under the rug.

I had a friend growing up whose mother and father divorced at an early age. The father was never around and the fact that he abandoned the family left the mother very bitter and discouraged. She would consume a lot of alcohol and was very abusive toward her kids. They walked around on egg shells because they didn't want to 'make mama mad.' She often told them that she didn't care what they did as long as they left her alone. Her brothers were in and out of the juvenile system and her sister became a teenage mother twice before the age of seventeen. They just had a really hard time. Nothing was ever dealt with and the problems continued to worsen. They were being raised by a reclusive mother. Their father, too, was reclusive in his absence.

The word reclusive means "avoiding people, seclusion, withdrawal and to be in solitude."2 People who parent from this perspective often have suppressed feelings of inadequacy. They want to be left alone and refuse to ask for help. This parent has experienced tremendous loss and disappointment that in order to confront the issue means they have to uncover a painful, infected and dis-eased sore.

It's inevitable that children raised by a reclusive parent will have intense brokenness as adults. Children may find themselves having a rescue mentality that will ultimately leave them feeling depleted. They may have uncontrolled anger and severe depression as a result of trying to make everyone happy... people pleasing.

If left unchecked, this pattern of reclusive parenting will manifest itself in the lives of one's children. In fact, reclusive parenting is more than likely the result of a generational curse already established in the family bloodline.

Exclusive Parenting

Exclusive Parenting is when parents are concerned with some issues involving their children, but not others. They may ensure that their child's chores are done at home, but not their homework. They may allow (and even assist) their child to engage in illegal activity because they are paying bills at home, and supplying the parent with financial means.

Exclusive parents pick and choose the areas to be concerned with and it is usually self-gratifying and self-serving. If it is self-serving to the parent, they will engage. If the child's behavior does not accommodate the parent, they will not engage.

Exclusive parents, usually, only engage in areas where they are most comfortable or have more expertise. They are not prone to seek out help when needed. They would rather just disengage. They are not unloving parents. They want the best for their children. They are often misinformed and short on options to meet the needs of their family. They may not have the education to help their child with their homework nor the funds to hire a tutor. It would be easier to just rely on the school, and older siblings or for the child to fend for themselves to get the educational help that they need.

Exclusive parents feel like their backs are against the wall and that they are frequently out of options. Generational curses have created a stronghold inhibiting them from moving beyond their present knowledge and skillset into the next level of challenge and ambiguity. Fear, too, is often a guiding affect for the exclusive parent.

Another form of exclusive parenting is when a parent favors one child over another, like we saw in the story of Rebekah and son, Jacob. Rebekah favored her son Jacob over Esau and manipulated Jacob to betray his older brother, Esau. By doing so, Rebekah, in essence, shut Esau out and excluded him from receiving his share of love and attention from her.

A movie that I love to watch from time to time, *Boyz in the Hood*,3 perfectly illustrates exclusive parenting. The story follows a single mother raising two boys in Compton, California. The older son is depicted as a juvenile delinquent as the movie begins with him stealing from a store. He continues this thuggish and gangster behavior even throughout young adulthood. The younger son, on the other hand, is mama's pride and joy. He's a stand-out football player and deemed the obvious and only chance for the family to ever escape the harmful realities and misfortunes of the hood.

In the movie, you see a strict contrast between the upbringing of the two boys. The son who's considered a thug appears to have little to no positive male interactions or intervention from any adult or community members except through penal institutionalization. The promising son, on the other hand, has a best friend, the main character, whose father is involved in the boys' lives, as they are neighbors. In one scene, the father takes the boys to his place of employment and talks with them about investments and other life issues. The boys appeared to have been enlightened by that experience and consider their future as a result of this conversation.

The story ends with the promising son being killed by gangsters of a different neighborhood, or sect. The mother's first response was to blame the gangster son for the death of her prized child, when in fact the troubled son was not the culprit of the atrocity.

In one scene, the troubled son had a conversation with a friend about his mother loving his brother more than him. His friends even noticed that the troubled son (Doughboy) had been excluded from his mother's love and attention. In the end, their troubling family dynamics continued to elevate. Doughboy was killed shortly afterward and although not shown, I'm sure his death and the death of his brother left their mother in a horrible state. I'm sure she dealt with grief, regret, unforgiveness and even self-hate.

I wonder what would have happened if the mother took a more proactive stance in her "troubled" son's life. Would the outcome have been different? I'm pressed to believe that his life could have been more positive with the proper interventions and love.

It's sometimes easier to turn a blind eye and ignore painful circumstances instead of taking challenges head-on. Maybe the mother had reached out to other people for help with raising her son, although this was never depicted in the story. It seemed that once he got in trouble, she gave up on raising him and trying to correct his behavior. She became exclusive, only focusing her attention on the promising son. She ignored Doughboy's cries for help and refused to get him the help he needed.

It's easier to recluse or exclude than it is to tighten up your bootstraps, roll up your sleeves and get into the fight. It's simpler to bury your heads in the sand hoping your problems will disappear than it is to take your problems head on. In good parenting, there is no other option, you have to determine in your mind that you are all in. You have to declare "come what may, I'm well able to see this thing through!"

Inclusive Parenting

Good parenting is inclusive parenting. That is, involvement in every aspect of your children's lives whether inconspicuously (because of their age and maturity) or conspicuously because of their lack thereof. Inclusive Parenting requires full engagement from parents through physical, emotional and/or spiritual means and support.

Inclusive parenting is being present, prayerful, patient and persistent in your children's lives, otherwise known as the Powerful P's of Inclusive Parenting. It requires a great deal of tact, love and sacrifice to do it well.

Rarely do we see this variance of parenting, but it's not uncommon. God Parents us through inclusive parenting and He enables us to raise ours in the same manner and to the best of our ability.

Inclusive parenting is not perfect parenting. No one gets it right all the time. What matters most is the determination one has, the persistence if you will, to try at it again even when you feel you've failed in some area. Failing at some things does not mean you are not inclusive in your parenting, it means you're human. When you are able to get back up and try to right some wrongs, you are being inclusive.

The Powerful P's of Inclusive Parenting

Presence

Inclusive Parenting demands presence! Presence is of utmost importance, not only to children, but to God. See Malachi's strict rebuke to Judah's priest concerning their unfaithfulness to their families:

"Another thing you do: You flood the LORD's altar with tears. You weep and wail because He no longer looks with favor on your offerings or accepts them with pleasure from your hands. You ask, "Why?" It is because the LORD is the witness between you and the wife of your youth. You have been unfaithful to her, though she is your partner, the wife of your marriage covenant. Has not the One God made you? You belong to Him in body and spirit. And what does the One God seek? *Godly offspring*. So be on your guard, and do not be unfaithful to the wife of your youth. "The man who hates and divorces his wife," says the LORD, the God of Israel, "does violence to the one he should protect," says the LORD Almighty. So be on your guard, and do not be unfaithful."[4]

One of the reasons God hates divorce is because it crushes a child's spirit. Kids are given no logical explanation as to why their family has been torn apart, and so they conjure up falsities to compensate for their lack of understanding.

When my son was younger, he shared with me that he thought the reason his father and I weren't together was because of him. He couldn't explain to me why he thought that, he just did. His perception, although farthest from the truth, he'd internalized, for God only knows how long. The enemy had planted that seed in his mind and it took some time to convince him otherwise.

I assured him, however, that he was the best thing that had happened to us and he's the reason why we have maintained a good co-parenting relationship thus far. Kids conjure up untruths when they are hurting and lack a mature understanding of adult issues. For this and other reasons, God has called parents to be faithful to one another and to be married.

But, life happens...

When my ex-husband and I divorced, I prayed vehemently that the effects of divorce be minimal for our son. Although, my parents never divorced, I knew that divorce could be very traumatic for kids. I understood that feelings of rejection and grief were soon to follow.

No matter how much you prepare, no one escapes the sting of divorce. God wouldn't be God if there was not a penalty for divorce and having kids out of wedlock. For when we do things out of the will of God, there are consequences. The best we can do is to try and minimize the harmful effects of divorce and unwed pregnancies, but we can't prevent all the suffering that comes along with sin.

God designed marriage for the whole family. Kids need both parents in their lives to be their best selves. I've had several conversations with men who believe that boys need to be raised by their father at a certain age, as if to say that mothers can't raise young men. Although boys do need fathers and male role models, kids are emotionally healthier when they receive love, support and full engagement from both parents. There are limits to what one parent can provide. True, fathers can teach a boy how to conduct himself properly, as a man. However, a mother, too, teaches her son how to be a gentleman and to love and care for a woman and children. A mother can teach her daughter how to conduct herself as a lady, but a father teaches her how to be loved, provided and cared for by a man. Children are not healthy and whole when parenting is one sided. They need a family (a village) in order to be healthy and whole.

I tried my best and sacrificed a lot to ensure that my son's father maintained a presence in our son's life, being that he lived hundreds of miles away. Thankfully, he always obliged, for he wanted to be there for Jai. Since distance was a factor, they would talk on the phone on most days. When Jai was out of school on holidays and other breaks, he traveled to be with his father in New York. There were times when Jai needed more attention from his father because of something he was going through or he just simply wanted him at a basketball game. He would showed up.

It was important for me, too, to always remind my son how much his father *and* I loved him. I never wanted him to feel unloved or abandoned by either of us. I didn't talk bad about his father regardless of what I felt about him.

When they had a disagreement, I reassured Jai that his dad had his best interest at heart.

I may have manipulated the narrative I shared with Jai concerning his father, a time or two. It was more important for me to train his mind to believe the best about his being raised by a single mother and the fact that his father was not physically present every day. The reality is, however, Jai still felt abandoned by his father because he simply was not around for much of his life. I, on the other hand felt like he was present enough and sometimes too much, lol.

The outcome of my manipulation is that the respect and love has always been present between Jai and his father and Jai no longer internalizes our divorce as being his fault. I've also found that the positivity and optimism has actually manifested itself in a pretty decent co-parenting relationship between his father and I, which has benefited us in those times when Jai needed disciplining.

We agreed several years ago, Jai's father and I, after countless arguments (which rarely occurred around our son) and a barrel of tears, that we would have each other's back as it pertained to disciplining Jai... for he was growing up and trying to play us against one another. He tried to outsmart the both of us, lol. But, we became a united front and shut him down early on, lol.

I know there are many people who are unable to maintain a healthy co-parent relationship with the absent parent, so you have to be very prayerful about it. Prayer can go where you cannot. It can change a heart. For the Bible tells us that God is "turning the hearts of the fathers back to the children and the hearts of the children to their fathers."[5] God is the only One who can change hearts. Our obligation is to take our matters and concerns to Him in prayer and to watch Him work them out for us, because prayer changes things and God is faithful.

work
p. 50

Presence in Every Stage of Life

Parents can and should be present in every stage of their children's lives, whether directly or indirectly. When children are young, we carry them. As they grow older, we let them walk on their own. They fall down, bump their heads and make many mistakes. They often learn through folly, which can be quite uncomfortable for parents. We don't want our kids to get hurt or make big mistakes. We want to protect and coddle them as much as we can... for as long as we can.

I remember being furious with my son for about a week when he was younger. I'd noticed that there was a quarter-sized burn mark on his bedroom ceiling. As you can imagine, I let him have it. I gave him the whole spill about "this is my house and you don't pay bills here... You bet' not ever light up anything else in this house, ever again" kind of deal.

Then, I asked him why he did it. He said that the design on the ceiling looked as if the paint was dripping, he wanted to see what would happen if he was to apply heat to it... Loooooong sigh... Thankfully, that was the first and last time that ever happened. Kids learn through folly, unfortunately, and if your child is anything like mine, he experiments and tries things out on occasion, smh.

Teenagers... teenagers work very hard to keep you out of their 'business.' Their lives are always highly-classified and ultra-sensitive. They're pretty good at what they do, but the Holy Spirit is wiser! It's during the teenage years that we must totally rely on the leading of the Holy Spirit to guide us in our decision-making because rarely will our kids disclose their lives to us and seek our advice.

Our presence in the teenager's life takes on a whole different meaning than when they were younger. Parents can't hover over teenagers, so presence requires skill. Planning meaningful time away with your kids, eating meals together at the dinner table and having a set time for family night, are all skillful ways to maintain a healthy presence in your teenager's life. Beware, though, because at first, they will resist your requests for dinner dates and outings. They won't want to play UNO with you. They may not allow you to play them on the video game the first time you ask, but stick with it. One day they will relent.

Luckily, you can pretty much tell what state of mind your teens are in by their attitudes. If you observe, you can tell when they are happy or have had a good day. You can also tell when they appear sad and distant, for they may want to be alone.

We know our kids, their friends and associates (for the most part), and we know when things aren't right. The Holy Spirit will lead and guide you to offer a kind word, a gentle touch or simply the unction to pray to help them make it through the tough times.

As a single mother I have always tried to stay on top of my son's emotional state, especially in his teenage years. I observe when he is sad, quieter and more reserved. It's in those times, I suggest he reach out to his father, or I may call his father and suggest that he call Jai and/or plan a visit to spend time with him soon. This is more than a notion, but I've found that usually hearing his father's voice makes a huge difference in my son's life.

Another solution I've found is to try to get him out of the house. Sometimes, just the change of scenery is enough to lighten his mood. That concept proves true for adults, too. Instead of obsessing over your problems, do something productive and before you know it, a solution or answer comes to you and you don't waste too much time worrying about something that God has already worked out anyways. All in all, you will have to find solutions that work best for your children.

This requires sacrifice. We tend to give kids what we think they need (or what we would need in their predicament) verses what they actually need. It's sometimes difficult to distinguish between the two, your need or theirs, but not impossible. The more time we spend with them, listening and just being present, we are able to discern more clearly the longings of their hearts.

For young adult children, particularly those away in college or the military, being present is nearly impossible. Please don't travel to see them every weekend or make a big fuss about them coming home to see you, LOL. Presence for this stage of life requires much prayer and frequent phone calls. Ask if you can pray with them on a particular issue or concern. Hopefully, then you can gain insight into what's going on in their lives. Also, ask questions about their interests. This is necessary in every stage of their lives. Do your best to see to it that you don't bash their interests, regardless of how senseless it may sound.

I recently had a conversation with one of my favorite uncles. He was going on about how he raised his daughter on his knees. From the time she was a baby until now, a grown, married woman with children, he has lived in another state. Although, he consistently paid child support and visited on a regular basis, he felt his greatest contribution to his daughter was his sincere prayer life which he cultivated from the beginning. He is seeing the fruit of those prayers today as she and her family are truly blessed. Again, prayer can go where we cannot. It can do what we can't. I can't explain how it works, only that it does. You really can win the battle for your kids on your knees.

Adult children find their way back to the security of a trusted parent. They want you to be present in their lives because they need babysitters, LOL. They have matured past the careless and carefree stage of life and are making better choices for themselves. They want advice and guidance as they begin to realize that they really don't know everything like they once thought they did.

Your role and relationship to your adult child takes on a new form. You are no longer running their lives nor are they obligated to follow your every word of advice. They are finding their own way and forging their own paths. They are living their lives the way in which they choose. Parents have to step off and trust God that what they have placed in their children, will manifest. Allow them to be adults! Encourage them to trust the God in them to lead them in the direction that they should go.

This was extremely difficult for my father (and sometimes my mother). I am the baby and sometimes I think they think I'm still 16 years old. My father lives by the ancient concept (or misconception, lol) that "father knows best." He wants you to do it his way and his way only. He had a hard time letting go.

I've found that if you relent from trying to force your ideologies and opinions upon your children and resist trying to control them, you'll find your adult children seeking your guidance more and more. You'll find that your kids actually listened to you and you will have peace.

Prayer is key! Parents must pray that they are able to release their children and that God will give them the grace to discern a need and to be able to meet the need without being burdensome, when given the opportunity to be present in their children's life.

Prayerful

Of course, it's impossible to effectively raise happy, healthy kids who love God without prayer... Much prayer! Prayer is the catalyst for effective inclusive parenting. The major premise for understanding the call to parent is knowing that God partners with you and comes alongside you to help you raise your children, for your children are His children whom

He has entrusted to your care. He will take care of them. God knows exactly what He's doing.

Prayer is important for every stage of your child's life. When they are in utero, we pray that we have healthy, cute (lol) children. When they are toddlers, we tend to pray for God to cover and protect them from predators. We also pray that they are smart and don't get into too much trouble.

I remember being a young mother with many fears. I would have this recurring dream that my son was kidnapped or lost somewhere. I would wake up in a cold sweat, having to pray that those things never ever happened.

Prayer is communing with God. It entails petitioning the Lord on behalf of yourself or another person. It's so powerful that each prayer prayed is stored in Heaven.[6] No prayer is ever wasted. When we pray, we're communing with a risen Savior, Who's touched by our infirmities. God cares about everything that concerns us. What we care about, God cares about.

As parents, we have an obligation *and a privilege* to seek the Lord for guidance with raising our children. It's our duty to prepare them for life and to be all that God created them to be. It's up to us to catapult them in the direction (of life) that they should go.[7] Much prayer produces the expected outcome.

Apart from obligation, what a privilege it is to have unlimited access to the One Who has all power and such great love for us! We are to follow Jesus' example as it pertains to prayer. The scriptures tell us that "Jesus often withdrew to lonely places and prayed."[8] He knew the importance of spending time alone with God. In order for him to be effective at completing the task He was called to do, He needed constant guidance from the Father.

There's an often-quoted church soliloquy that says "No Prayer, No Power. Some Prayer, Some Power. Much Prayer, Much Power!" In single parenting, we need much power. The more time we spend in prayer with the Father, the more we experience God's provision in our lives.

My son and I have established a weekly custom of praying together on Sunday nights (before bed). I don't want to hover over him and demand that he prays, I just want him to have an authentic relationship with God, through prayer. It's very important to me that he experiences us setting aside time to honor and commune with the Father, as a family... if only for a few moments.

I also frequently utilize my son as my prayer partner. I may share a prayer concern with him and ask if he will agree with me in prayer. He has yet to turn me down when I present it to him in this way. I also report back with a praise report when our prayers are answered.

Sometimes, we are fortunate enough to have our children share their concerns with us. That has been a rare occurrence in my house but not obsolete. I always try to first encourage my son to pray about his concerns and then I may offer advice. In his immaturity, he doesn't always think that prayer is the answer. But, one day he will.

I believe I am training him or helping him to develop his own prayer life. I want him to trust God above all else. He needs to know that apart from God, he can do nothing.

Many kids are not inclined to put their trust in God because they have everything they want. They don't have to believe for anything because the parents are always giving them the desires of their little feeble hearts. I'm guilty of this, too. Kids can, however, learn to trust God. Parents can ignite this desire by praying for this desire. God's got it covered from there.

Patience

Loooong sigh...

We pray and we wait on the manifestation of our prayer requests.

In the waiting stage, we trust God and continue to work. That means we continue the process of raising happy, healthy kids who love God even when there's very little to no change. We attend PTA meetings, we help our kids with homework, take them to church, spend time with them, involve them in meaningful activities and we discipline them as needed.

Patience is not stagnation. It's not doing nothing and expecting change. In fact, I propose that patience is actually discipline. God is always disciplining us to conform to His image and likeness. It's not an easy feat because we are quite stubborn. We want things done the way we want them. We want to be the masters of our fate. We don't want to conform to another pattern of life, except that which is familiar to us.

Change rarely comes easy and it doesn't always look like God is working on our behalf. It's in those times that we have to be disciplined enough through the reading of the Word, prayer, fasting (sometimes), serving and uniting with a local church, to increase our faith and remain steadfast. Because inclusive parenting is challenging.

I believe Haggai 2:1-9 illustrates this appropriately: "The word of the Lord came by Haggai the prophet, saying: 2 "Speak now to Zerubbabel the son of Shealtiel, governor of Judah, and to Joshua the son of Jehozadak, the high priest, and to the remnant of the people, saying: 3 'Who is left among you who saw this house in its former glory? And how do you see it now? In comparison with it, *is this* not in your eyes as nothing? 4 Yet now be strong, Zerubbabel,' says the Lord; 'and be strong, Joshua, son of Jehozadak, the high priest; and be strong, all you people of the land,' says the Lord, 'and work; for I *am* with you,' says the Lord of hosts. 5 '*According to* the word that I covenanted with you when you came out of Egypt, so My Spirit remains among you; do not fear!'

6 "For thus says the Lord of hosts: 'Once more (it *is* a little while) I will shake heaven and earth, the sea and dry land; 7 and I will shake all nations, and they shall come to the Desire of All Nations, and I will fill this temple with glory,' says the Lord of hosts. 8 'The silver *is* Mine, and the gold *is* Mine,' says the Lord of hosts. 9 'The glory of this latter house shall be greater than the former,' says

the Lord of hosts. 'And in this place, I will give peace,' says the Lord of hosts."

Parenting, done well, can have extremely long and delayed gratification. Seems we give more than we receive. We work hard with little to no thanks or acknowledgment... especially single parents. But, there will come a day when you will receive your due diligence, if you stay the course and wait on God.

A common saying in the black church goes "He may not come when you want Him, but He's always on time." We can't predict when the Lord will show up in our situation. Our job is to trust Him and remain faithful to the Call. Have patience! God will indeed show up! "They that wait upon the Lord shall renew their strength. They shall mount up on wings as eagles. They shall run and not be weary. They shall walk and not faint."9 One day, you will clearly see the manifestation of your prayers. Your hard work of inclusive single parenting will pay off in the end and "the glory of your latter house will be greater than your former!"10

Persistence
Don't ever give up! Not on yourself, or your children. Stay the course. Sure, it will take time to see the full manifestation of your hard work, but it will manifest. God is faithful!

The great globetrotter, the Apostle Paul, who endured many adversities on his way to the manifestation of the fulfillment of the promises of God wrote in Philippians 3:14, "I press toward the goal for the prize of the high calling of God in Christ Jesus."11 Paul is reminding us to stay focused on the goal. We are raising happy, healthy kids who love

God! We can't be swayed to and fro by the vicissitudes of life and adversity. We have many great promises and we will see them manifested in our lives, if we stay the course.

Sure, there will be difficult and challenging days. There will be some sleepless nights. You will shed a tear or two. But, rest assured that payday is coming because nothing is permanent and seasons do change.

"One day Jesus told his disciples a story to show that they should always pray and never give up. "There was a judge in a certain city," he said, "who neither feared God nor cared about people. A widow of that city came to him repeatedly, saying, 'Give me justice in this dispute with my enemy.' The judge ignored her for a while, but finally he said to himself, 'I don't fear God or care about people, but this woman is driving me crazy. I'm going to see that she gets justice, because she is wearing me out with her constant requests!'"

Then the Lord said, "Learn a lesson from this unjust judge. Even he rendered a just decision in the end. So, don't you think God will surely give justice to his chosen people who cry out to him day and night? Will he keep putting them off? I tell you, he will grant justice to them quickly! But when the Son of Man[a] returns, how many will he find on the earth who have faith?"[12]

God wants us to trust Him. Pray. Stand on His Word. Remain faithful! Faithful to the call. Faithful to trust. Faithful to believe HIM!

Get in the fight to save your children. Your battle may not be like mine, but the same God has given us all His great promises. And "He Who promises, is Faithful!"13 He will come through for you!

It's my prayer that we all work smarter at being inclusive parents. Our Heavenly Father is inclusive! He loves us all the same. He sent His Son Jesus for us all. He's concerned with every detail of our being. He's not a smotherer (or controlling), for He has given us all freewill and the opportunity to make our own choices. But God promises to always be there. He sometimes walks beside us. Other times, He goes before us. There are even times when He has to carry us. But, He's always there... always guiding, providing, disciplining and comforting us. What an honor it is to be made in the image and likeness of Him.

Chapter 5: *Abba, Father!*

"A Father of the fatherless, a defender of widows, Is God in His holy habitation."

Psalm 68:5

In the Old Testament of the Bible there are numerous names or titles of God that help us to better understand the nature and character of God. These titles also help us to understand God's role in our lives and our significance to Him as His children. These same attributes offer a design for parenting. We will discuss several of them in this chapter and glean from Him, as we develop our own parenting methodology.

Jehovah Shammah

Jehovah Shammah, my favorite God-name, means 'the Lord is there' in Hebrew. One can interpret 'the Lord is there' to mean that God is always with us. It could also have a future connotation, meaning, that wherever we go, God is already there and has made provision for us.

We first see this reference in Ezekiel 48:35 when the Lord shows Ezekiel the gates around the city of Jerusalem. Gates we know provide safety and security for people. God told Ezekiel that the entire city would be called, Jehovah Shammah. That meant that whenever anyone talked about, entered, or wanted to siege the city of Jerusalem, they would have to weigh their decisions under the pretense of contending with Jehovah Shammah, because the Lord is there.

In Antiquity, when folks went into battle with one another, the persons or tribe that won the battle was believed to have the more powerful god. The Israelites had a reputation of having the most powerful God.

God was showing Ezekiel how He would always protect the city. He was promising to always be there and to watch over them. A few years ago, my son and I were outside late at night watching a 'Blood Moon.' While the clouds were moving in and out they formed the shape of a hand right above our house. It was the most amazing sight to behold. Overjoyed, I snapped all kinds of photos to remind myself that God's Hand was indeed over my family. There have been a few traumatic events pertaining to my home, but God protected us through it all. Truly, "no weapon formed against us has been able to prosper, for the Lord is with us."[1]

God's method of parenting is Inclusive. He's always there. He gets in the trenches with us so that we are never alone. "He promises to never leave us, nor forsake us."[2] We, too, can bring assurance to our kids that we will be there for them in their time of need. They need to know that they are protected by a competent, loving parent. We must let them know that we will never give up on them regardless of the circumstances.

El Roi

"The God Who Sees." I love this God-Title because it lets us know that when it seems no one cares, God knows and He cares. The pregnant Hagar, who we read about in chapter 1, gave God this name as she fled from her abusive mistress, Sarah (see Genesis 16).

Hagar's life was always under submission to abuse and control. There was no wedding proposal, yet she became Abraham's concubine. There was no sexual consent, but she became pregnant. Hagar was always at the beck and call of her mistress, Sarah, and whenever Sarah wanted to use and abuse Hagar, she did. But, what I love about God is that when Hagar tried to flee, He went after her. How often do we wish someone would come running after us, rescuing us, fighting for us and even asking for another chance?!

God sent an angel to reassure Hagar that He saw what she was going through and that He would take care of her. The Angel of the Lord told Hagar in verse 10, to go back and be faithful to her mistress, Sarah, and that He would "increase [her] descendants that they would be too numerous to count." In other words, God was letting Hagar know that there was still glory in her story. Although it felt like the end, it wasn't the end. There was greater to come for her!

God's revealing of Himself to Hagar and giving her His Word assured that she would be alright and that there was purpose in her pain. God promised her a good future.

God had a plan for Hagar and He has a plan for you. It doesn't matter who you are, where you've been, what you've done, or the manner in which you did it. God has a plan for you. He can use your most adverse situation for His Glory.

God let Hagar know that He was well-aware of what she was going through... He saw her. I've heard many children say that they feel so alone and often misunderstood by the adults in their lives. They think that what they are going through others would never understand. They need to know that many of the same challenges they are facing, other adults have already experienced. We've been there, done that and got a t-shirt. The challenge, then, is for parents to allow themselves to be vulnerable enough to share with their kids some of their own life lessons.

Just imagine how much better your kid's life would be if they had someone with experience in the area of their struggle. Well, they do! You are the expert. God has brought you through tumultuous things so that you can help them make it through theirs.

Adults are usually pros at offering advice to their friends, co-workers, church members, family and neighbors. We can tell our girlfriends what they should do, all day long. Yet, we are sometimes challenged and at a loss for words when it comes to giving our kids advice based off of our own life experiences... especially the really painful ones. But they, too, need to know how you overcame your life's adversities, so that they can overcome.

Sometimes, kids just want to know that you see what they are going through. They want you to care about what they care about. In God's inclusivity, He constantly assures us that He sees us and He cares. He's concerned with everything that concerns us.

Jehovah Jireh

Perhaps, one of the most common names of God found in the Hebrew Bible is Jehovah Jireh, or Yahweh Yireh in Hebrew. This God-Name means, "The Lord Will Provide." The Name, given by Abraham, represents the place on Mount Moriah where Abraham was instructed by God to sacrifice his son of the promise, Isaac.

Gory as it sounds, God was testing Abraham's love and devotion to Him. And at just the right time, before Abraham sacrificed his son, Isaac, *God provided* a ram to be killed instead. Thus, the name Jehovah Jireh.

Jehovah Jireh is echoed from the pulpits of America and throughout the world on any given Sunday. Reference is made to the unchanging fact that God always provides for His people.

A great challenge for many single parents is figuring out how you will make ends meet day after day. Having the same responsibilities as a married couple, but not the financial means of a two-parent household, it's very difficult to raise happy, healthy kids who love God and to live the abundant life God promised. I don't care how you wrap it, two incomes are always better than one. In fact, the Word tells us that two of everything is always better than one. It says in Ecclesiastes 4:9-12, "two are better than one;

because they have a good reward for their labor. For if they fall, one will lift up his companion. But, woe to him who is alone when he falls, for he has no one to help him up. Again, if two lie down together, they will keep warm; But how can one be warm alone? Though one may be overpowered by another, two can withstand him. And a threefold cord is not easily broken."3

The good news is that single parents are never really alone. God is always there providing for us. I joke a lot that my son thinks he is Richie Rich because sometimes he thinks money grows on trees. He hasn't seen all the payment arrangements I've had to make. He has no clue of all the robbing Peter to pay Paul that I've done.

Kids just don't know the extent of our sacrifice and what it takes to be a good, single parent. They don't fully understand the struggle because good, single parents make parenting look easy. We always make a way out of no way, especially for our children. Tupac said, "Mama made miracles every Thanksgiving."4 LOL. I beg to differ... With the help of the Lord, single parents make miracles every day! We may not always know when we will receive our blessing, but, we know the Source and He continuously provides.

Matthew 6:25-34 says, "Therefore I tell you, do not worry about your life, what you will eat or drink; or about your body, what you will wear. Is not life more than food, and the body more than clothes? Look at the birds of the air; they do not sow or reap or store away in barns, and yet your heavenly Father feeds them. Are you not much more valuable than they? Can any one of you by worrying add a single hour to your life? And why do you worry about clothes? See how the flowers of the field grow. They do not labor or spin. Yet I tell you that not even Solomon in all his splendor was dressed like one of these. If that is how God clothes the grass of the field, which is here today and tomorrow is thrown into the fire, will he not much more clothe you—you of little faith? So, do not worry, saying, 'What shall we eat?' or 'What shall we drink?' or 'What shall we wear?' For the pagans run after all these things, and your heavenly Father knows that you need them. But seek first his kingdom and his righteousness, and all these things will be given to you as well. Therefore, do not worry about tomorrow, for tomorrow will worry about itself. Each day has enough trouble of its own."[5] Whatever the need, Jehovah Jireh promises to always provide for us.

Jehovah Rapha

Found in Exodus 15:26, the Israelites, after their exodus from Egypt, wandered in the Desert of Shur for three days without water. When they finally reached Marah, the water there was too bitter to drink.[6] They cried out to God and He showed Moses a piece of wood to place in the water to sweeten it, allowing the Israelites to drink from it. It was there that God revealed Himself as Jehovah Rapha, 'The Lord Who Heals.'

I don't know what it was about my parent's bed when I was a little girl, but whenever I was sick, I wanted to lay in it to feel better. I noticed that I slept better and recovered faster sleeping in their bed. At least that's what I told myself.

In all actuality, parents do have a healing touch to soothe and comfort their children. We can also say the right words to calm a child's anxiety and to drive away fear. Our peaceful homes, our gentle touch, our loving presence and encouraging words are all effective tools that God gives us to heal our families.

If we will just call on Him, He'll sweeten the waters of our lives, for He is the Healer. He's always trying to bring us to a place of wholeness in Him. His plan is that we "prosper and be in health, even as our souls prosper."[7]

Abba, Father!
Jesus called on 'Abba, Father' in the Garden of Gethsemane, found in Mark 14. The scriptures tell us that Jesus was severely anguished in His Spirit, for it was time that He would be crucified for the sins of humanity. It was in His distress that He cried out, "Abba, Father, everything is possible for you. Take this cup from Me."[8] Jesus wanted His Father to rescue Him from the persecution that He would soon endure, even death on the cross. Thankfully, and to our benefit, Jesus went on to say "Yet, not My will, by Thy will be done," proving His total trust in His Father's perfect plan.

Abba is an Aramaic word that simply means "Father, or Daddy."[9] This title refers to the most intimate relationship between a father and child. Picture a young girl clinging to her father when she is afraid and you will see a pictorial of Abba, Father. The father, then, represents the safest, most secured dwelling for the child.

Jesus' reference to 'Abba Father' signifies the relationship that He had with His Father. He wanted God to rescue Him as God had done every time in the past. Many theologians suggest that this was the first of two times when Jesus *felt* abandoned by His Father. The second time being on the cross when Jesus cried out, "My God, My God, why has Thou forsaken Me."[10]

Often times, we find ourselves in trouble and we need the Lord to rescue us in the same manner that He has done before. However, God is a Disciplinarian and what's more important to Him is that we learn the lessons needed for us to accomplish what He's called us to do. God uses tests and trials to discipline us for His service. It's through discipline that we are made strong. We learn how to fight when we endure some pain and suffering. The Word tells us that "who God loves, He chastises, or disciplines."[11] We have to go through times of uncertainty and challenge in order to find out what we're made of. The only true way to know whether or not we are fit for the fight is to fight.

I've found that on this Christian journey, we are actually trained while in battle. While in the fight we learn what's inside of us... or rather Who is inside of us. Once we figure that out, we learn how to win.

I remember a time when my mother wanted me to talk with a friend of hers who was a Jehovah's Witness about the Bible. I agreed to do so because I felt I was proficient in the Word of God. Little did I know, I was still a babe in Christ as the woman ran circles around my knowledge of Scripture and theology. I thought to myself, "that will never happen again. I'm getting into my Word so that the next time we battle, I'll be ready for her. LOL." Because I hate to lose.

Thankfully, that wasn't a true battle for "we wrestle not against flesh and blood."12 Although, there have been plenty of real battles that I've had to fight. I've found that all of those battles were fixed. I already had the victory. I only needed to know who I was and Whose I am. Battles catapult us into our destiny and our even greater purpose. Because Abba Father loves us so deeply and so richly, He's always leading us to our greater purpose.

The Spirit of Adoption
We find the title, 'Abba, Father,' again in Romans 8:15. Paul said, "For ye have not received the spirit of bondage again to fear; but ye have received the Spirit of adoption, whereby we cry, Abba, Father."13

The **Spirit of Adoption** refers to the spiritual nature we receive when we accept Jesus Christ as our Lord and Savior. Before we come to know Christ, or as church-folk like to say, "while we are yet in sin," we are slaves to sin. We do whatever the flesh desires. Technically, we are under the law of sin and death for death is the consequence of sin. However, when we receive the free gift of salvation, found only in Jesus Christ, we not only receive eternal life,14 but we also become the sons and daughters of God, or as Paul puts it, 'Heirs of God and joint heirs with Christ."15 That means we have all the blessings, rights and privileges as the Son.

Think about adoption in the natural sense. When a family or parent adopts a child, the child is no longer a ward of the state or belonging to someone else. They now become a part of their new family. In the same manner, when we accept Jesus as our Lord and Savior, we no longer belong to satan nor are we subjected to serving him any longer. We now belong to Christ.

When a child is adopted, they have the same rights and privileges as natural children... including the inheritance of the Father. When we become heirs of God, we receive what belongs to the Father. Jesus said in Matt. 11:27, "All things have been committed to Me by My Father." John 5:22-23 says, "Moreover, the Father judges no one, but has entrusted all judgment to the Son, that all may honor the Son just as they honor the Father. Whoever does not honor the Son does not honor the Father, who sent Him." Putting this into context, if, then, we are joint heirs with Christ, meaning we have the same rights and privileges as Christ, then we, too, have this level of influence. God is for us and "if God is for us, who can be against us?" 16

The prerequisite for being called the sons and daughters of God is to "suffer with Christ." Paul said in Romans 8:17, "And *if* children, then heirs; heirs of God, and joint-heirs with Christ; *if so be that we suffer with him,* that we may be also glorified together." Suffering with Christ means that we carry our cross and endure hardships with total faith in Daddy God.

Carrying one's cross means to be obedient and fully submitted to the plan of God for your life. This is not always an easy task and can sometimes require more of you than you are willing to give, but Jesus promises that when we go with Him all the way, we will also share in His glory. And, we all love the glory of God.

A Prayer of Salvation

Abba, Father is always longing for a deep, intimate relationship with you. If you don't know Jesus in the pardoning of your sins, you are not privy to the glory of God and all of His benefits. You can't access the inheritance if you aren't in the family. However, having a personal relationship with Abba, Father is as easy as quoting these words aloud:

"Lord Jesus, I am a sinner. Today I repent of my sins, especially the sin(s) of (state them aloud). I want you to come into my life. I want to follow You. Lord, I need you to show me how to do things Your way. I believe that You died on the cross for my sins and that You rose on the third day so that I may have eternal life. Jesus, I receive You as my Lord and Savior and I surrender my will to Yours. Thank you for the precious gift of salvation."

If you prayed that prayer in faith, believing in your heart on the Lord Jesus Christ, YOU ARE SAVED! Welcome to the Body of Believers! I encourage you to A.S.S.E.S.S.TM your family's spiritual needs (read more about that in chapter seven) and then find a community of Bible Believers who preach and teach the unadulterated Word of God.

Know that this Christian walk is a marathon and not a sprint. There will be challenging seasons and seasons of great victories. Know that you are blessed regardless of the season you are in! Remain faithful to "suffer with Him" so that you can share in His Glory! It's all yours because you are God's heir and co-heirs with Christ.

Chapter 6: *Live the Abundant Life NOW!*

"I have come that they might have life, and that they may have it more abundantly."

John 10:10

Fulfilling the Call to Parent requires that you take good care of yourself. Your children are depending on you being a happy, healthy parent who loves God, when considering their own well-being. In order to be an inclusive parent, you must be healthy and whole. That means that you are healthy physically, mentally and spiritually, as much as you are able to control. It means that you have a good balance and understand what it means to enjoy the abundant life that God promised you.

One thing that I love about my parents is that they understood the need for balance in our lives. We went to church on Sunday mornings and on many Wednesdays, we attended Bible Study. My sister and I always participated in church plays and programs especially during Christmas and Easter season. We even went to revivals. We were raised to put God first. You were not allowed in my parent's house to hang out on Saturday night and not go to church on Sunday morning, I don't care how old you were. You were getting your butt up and going to church, lol.

My parents also understood the need to find enjoyment in other areas of your life as well. I was a cheerleader and, in a girl's, social group called U.B.U. which stands for Unique Babes Unlimited, lol. I had a social life. I was able to attend parties and hang with my friends on a regular basis. My friends and I would spend the night at each other's houses because our parents knew each other and trusted the parents of my friends.

My parents too would get together with their friends on occasion. The adults would be in one area of the house having a good time and the children would be someone else having a good time. It's impossible to raise happy, healthy kids when you don't enjoy your own life. If you are always taking care of children, cooking and cleaning, helping with homework, doing hair, folding laundry, you are not living the abundant life Christ died for you to live. You've got to get your passion back. You've got to get your joy back.

Remember "the blessing of the Lord maketh rich and adds no sorrow."1 God has placed too much inside of you for you to be sorrowful at home, meeting the needs of everyone else while neglecting yourself. The devil is a liar! It's time to live the abundant life that God has for you!

Get your stuff back! God not only created your kids for a specific purpose, but YOU also! God created you for His purpose and He's still expecting you to become all that He created you to be. It's not too late. You haven't missed out on much at all but, you have to determine to live your best life now. You got this because God's got you. Live the abundant life NOW!

A Dream Deferred

It's so easy for parents, especially single parents, to get caught up in the day to day hustle and bustle of life for life is so congested, on most days. We're so busy doing for others and taking care of kids that we often forget to care for ourselves.

When we were young, most of us had dreams and aspirations of becoming someone great. We had plans on changing the world and making a difference in other people's lives, and somewhere down the line, we got stuck in mediocrity and in a place where dreams go to die.

When I was a kid, I imagined I'd be a child psychologist/psychiatrist. I wanted to help kids successfully navigate throughout the nasty and difficult stages of life. I had a heavy burden of wanting to help people who couldn't seem to help themselves.

I remember wanting to befriend a girl who had recently lost her mother. It was as if I was in some way deeply experiencing sorrow and grief for her. So much so, I had my mother drive me to the wake so that I could be there to support her.

On another occasion, our local newspaper ran an article titled, *Student's Dream Vacations*. This article featured my 4th grade class at Edgewood Elementary School, in Anderson, Indiana. While other kids wrote about going to

Disney World and traveling to visit their grandparents, I wrote about going to Africa to help kids who were less-fortunate.

I never became that child psychologist nor a therapist but, I've been teaching for twenty years in the public school with a concentration on at-risk, underserved student populations. I've also been in ministry for about fifteen years, thus far. I know that I'm doing what the Lord created me for and called me to do.

I'm a lifelong learner. When my son was born, I was in school working on my special education certification, while working at an alternative school in Greensboro, North Carolina. After my ex-husband and I split up, I moved back home to Indiana where I again felt the urge to enroll in school. This time for ministry.

When my son was very young and while working full-time as a special education teacher at an alternative school, I enrolled in Christian Theological Seminary in Indianapolis, Indiana to obtain my Master of Divinity. Working full-time and the obligation to complete ninety credit hours, it took me five years to complete that degree. My son was a 6th grader by the time I graduated. I again returned to school (two years later) and obtained my school administration license from Marian University in Indianapolis, Indiana.

That's a lot of schooling and certainly not recommended, lol while single parenting a young child. It's only by the grace of God... and the fact that I have one child, lol, that I was able to accomplish it all. I had a good support system (for the most part), people who believed in the God in me and were willing to come along side my journey and to help me out. Glory to God!

If you're not living your best life as a result of unfulfilled dreams, it's never too late to get back out there. You can still become the person that God created you to be. Pick up that paint brush, open that laptop and create a masterpiece, find a local tennis club and dust off your racket. Start that million-dollar business with the vision God gave you. Start selling the make-up line and hair care products you whipped up in your kitchen. Whatever your dream may be... Wherever your passion lies, now is the time to go for it! One day you will wake up and your kids will be gone enjoying their lives and fulfilling their dreams. Why not you too?! Journey with them on the road to become all that God created you to be and to live the abundant life that God promised. You'll be glad you did.

I've found that it's only in living out your purpose... doing what God has called you to do, that you will ever find true contentment and joy. Don't let finances, age, naysayers, fears, doubts or anything else stop you from fulfilling your call and purpose in life. Know that God will provide for you and your children. He's Jehovah Jireh and He'll take care of you!

Overcoming Fear

FEAR! Everything about the word just upsets me, lbvs (laughing but very serious). Probably because it was such a dominating force in my life... for most of my life. As a child, I would have this recurring dream, where I would be running (in slow motion) from someone or something chasing me. In my dream, I'd fall down unable to get back up. I'd wake up so afraid. To this day, I'm unaware of who or what was chasing me for, I was never captured. Never saw a face. Just afraid. And running.

Fear will do that to you. It'll have you running from and debilitated by a thought of something happening that will most likely never ever occur. Fear will have you running from something that truly doesn't exist. For, fear is an illusion.

I believe David said it best in Psalm 23:4 when he said, "Ye, though I walk through the valley of the *shadow of death*, I will fear no evil for thou art with me." David understood that the things we face, as long as we're walking with God, pose no real threat to our lives.

To be clear, fear *is* a healthy affect so long as it is momentary. The Lord gave fear to us so that we can be alerted to danger and harm. We need to know when something's not right so that we can avoid it. Fear can be a healthy response to an external danger.

I ran in my dream because I believed something was chasing me, but there was never anyone chasing me. I later realized that I was running from myself... The fear of possibilities. I was running from my potential... Running from who God created me to be. And, I continued to run for most of my adulthood.

If similar dreams plagued you as a child, I believe you, too, have a calling on your life. You have creativity and potential beyond your wildest dream and God wants to use you for His Glory. The fear you're experiencing is only the enemy trying to disrupt what God has placed on the inside of you. The sooner you accept the truth about who you are and Whose you are, you will soar as an eagle to your greatest potential.

A woman I knew always wanted to become a fashion designer. Ever since she was a little girl that was her dream. Her family, however, had other plans for her life and constantly pressured her to pursue less desirable professions. They even convinced her that pursuing her dream was senseless and would be unfruitful. Out of fear of failure and family rejection, she pursued meaningless, unfulfilling jobs. It wasn't until she overcame her fear of rejection and failure that she began to walk in her purpose and lead a more fulfilling life.

2 Timothy 1:7 says that "God has not given us a *spirit of fear* but of power, love and a sound mind."₂ Having a spirit of fear is an unhealthy, debilitating emotional state which is not of God. It's from the enemy. Its objective is to overtake and paralyze you from doing something, from stepping out on faith, and to stop you from becoming who God has created you to be. Spirits of fear are not of God and should not be entertained by Christians. God has promised us good things and fear is not one of them. Fear is your enemy.

Overcoming fear has been one of, if not the toughest battle of my life. For as long as I can remember, fear has reared its ugly head in almost every facet of my being-marriage, parenting, career, health and even some relationships. I've spent more time afraid of what *could* happen instead of trusting God that whatever happens, "is working for my good"3 and that I win every battle, so long as I trust Him.

In 2006, a heavy feeling of doom came upon me. I was afraid that I would lose my son. Nothing was wrong with him. There were no real threats on his life. Just out of nowhere the enemy posed those thoughts to me and I took the bait and became terribly afraid. He used my past in an attempt at stopping me from becoming all that God had called me to be.

You see, a few years prior to having my son, my daughter, Amani Anyé, passed away at six months old. She had a congenital heart defect. The enemy tried to use her death to plant fear in my heart concerning my son. And for a good little while, it worked. I became deeply depressed and saddened. A spirit of fear had come upon me.

I was so afraid of losing my son. It got to the point that I said, "what's the point of life if there's going to be so much sadness and pain?" Although I wasn't suicidal, I could of very well have checked out on life, at that time. I could have given up. That's what the enemy wanted me to do. Satan wanted me to become a hermit and reclusive, forfeiting the call of God on my life. He wanted to prevent my son and I from living the abundant life that Jesus promised me.

My bout with serious depression lasted for about a month until I decided that I would no longer be controlled by the enemy, or a spirit of fear. I acknowledged that I had too much Word on the inside of me to allow the devil to steal my joy. I declared at that moment that the enemy would NEVER EVER steal ANYTHING or ANYONE ELSE from me AGAIN... including my joy.

I began to speak the Word of God against the enemy, and even against my own thought-life. Whenever thoughts of doom and gloom would arise, I would speak aloud:

"I'm blessed in the city. Blessed in the field. Blessed when I go in. Blessed when I go out. The fruit of my womb is blessed, so Jai is blessed. My storehouses are blessed, so my bank account is blessed. All the works of my hands are blessed & everything I do, prospers, in Jesus' Name. I AM the head and not the tail, above and not beneath. I'm a lender and not a borrower. God has not given me a spirit of fear, but of power, love and a sound mind. Greater is He that is within me, than he that is in the world. I'm more than a conqueror through Christ who loves me. I have the mind of Christ. I can decree a thing and it will be established. He was wounded for my transgressions, bruised for my iniquities. The chastisement of my peace was upon Him and by His stripes, I'm healed. With long life He will satisfy us and show us His salvation. There is therefore now no condemnation for them who are in Christ Jesus. I'm redeemed from the course of the law and sin and death. God's plans are to prosper me and not to harm me, to give me hope and an expected end."

Whenever, I felt afraid, I would quote that same declaration aloud until I believed every word of it. Soon, those thoughts subsided. Jesus tells us to "resist the enemy and he will flee." We have to resist the urge to fear or worry because God's got us and everything will be alright.

When I came out of that pit of destruction, I began to walk in my calling as a minister of this great Gospel. I founded a women's empowerment ministry, Grace's Mercy Seat, Inc., in Indianapolis, Indiana, November 2006.

The enemy knows our potential and he knows our weaknesses. He sees the greatness the Lord has placed on the inside of us. He knows that if we ever get free, our whole family will be free, our loved ones will be free, our communities will get free, the nation and even the world.

Your story may not be my story but fear is still fear. Refuse to allow fear to control another second of your life. Don't let Satan steal another precious moment of enjoying your kids. If fear was not a factor, what would you do? Who would you become?

Know that you are powerful beyond measure. With Jesus Christ as your partner, you can do the impossible. You can make an impact on your family, your community & even the world. When you are walking in your God-given purpose, lives are changed, bodies are healed, faith is restored, and your children become happy, healthy kids who love God.

Guilt, Condemnation & Shame
Guilt by definition is "the fact or state of having done something wrong, or having committed a crime."4 We've all been guilty of doing something wrong at some point in our lives. We may have lied to our parents, stolen from a store, taken materials from the office, lied on our taxes, or cheated

on a spouse/mate. Whatever your sin may be, "we've all sinned and fallen short of the glory of God."[5]

When we sin, we can repent, or ask God to forgive us of our sins, and He will do it. For the Word tells us that "when we confess our sins, God is faithful and just to forgive us and to cleanse us from all unrighteousness."[6] Because Jesus has paid the ultimate price, the penalty for our sins, by death on the cross, we can dust ourselves off and get back in the race when we fall down. Now, considering the circumstances, there may be man-imposed penalties. However, with God, we can have a clean slate. That's what's most important.

Admitting guilt, or confession, is a healthy response to an injustice. It can alleviate confusion and pain. When we acknowledge guilt, we allow the healing, or cleansing process to begin as aforementioned in Scripture.

Condemnation, on the other hand, is an unhealthy and ungodly response to sin. Paul reminds us in Romans 8:1 that "there is therefore now no condemnation for them who are in Christ Jesus." When we sin, we repent and get back up. We are not to live under a cloud of guilt, fear or condemnation. We can rest assured that our sins are forgiven.

I've found that a lot of single parents struggle with guilt and condemnation by not being healed from their past. Condemnation is "the act of being condemned or sentenced to punishment." It also means, "to be judged unfit for use or service."[7] When a house is condemned it's completely destroyed and torn down. We, on the other hand, are never unfit for use or service nor are we completely destroyed. It may feel like the things we're going through are so destructive that there's no redemption, but that is a lie from the pits of hell. We always have a chance to make it right, as long as we have breath in our bodies. We still have "hope and a future."[8]

It's important that we don't let the mistakes and bad decisions from our past prevent us from enjoying the journey on the way to our future. We still have a bright future.

I'm reminded of a popular character on an old cartoon favorite, Pig-Pen from Charlie Brown. Pig-Pen had a cloud of dirt that followed him wherever he went. Regardless of what he did- showered or played in a rainstorm, he never could shake the dirt, literally. He even coined himself a "dirt magnet."[9] I'd like to propose that Pig-Pen suffered from condemnation. He could never envision his situation changing. Being dirty and unworthy, he assumed was his lot in life. His own words and behaviors provoked others to see him in the light in which he saw himself.

The same is true for us when we live life condemned. We exude sorrow and self-hatred. We live our lives stuck under a cloud of dirty laundry. At some point we have to let it go. Holding on to the guilt and shame from the past hinders a mighty move of God in our lives.

I'll be the first to admit that like Pig-Pen, it's hard to shake the dirt, sometimes. I've struggled with low self-esteem and have not always had a healthy self-image. I've had a failed marriage, buried a child, had a miscarriage, foreclosed on a home, sustained abandonment and a lot of rejection as well as a slew of other misfortunes. I have to constantly remind myself that I am who God says that I am. I have to encourage myself to know that God still loves me with an unfailing love & that He still has an awesome plan for my life.

To relish on anything other than the truth of God's Word which tells us who we are, is a waste of time and energy. Only what God says about us matters. And, he's called us the "apple of His eye."10 We may feel worthless, but God says we are valuable.11 Regardless of what we've done, God still wants to use us for His Glory. He still wants to give us "beauty for ashes."12

I will admit that it sometimes feels like I'm being punished for all the wrong I've done. When I have those thoughts, I have to quickly refute them and remind myself of who I am in Christ Jesus, or better yet, who He is in my life.

I've seen God work things out for my good. God has vindicated me, even when I've been wrong. He's shown me that I don't have to be perfect for Him to love me and to show me His favor. His love never fails. It never gives up on me. His "Grace is sufficient."13

Shame too, is another emotion that prevents us from effectively fulfilling the call of God on our lives. I've heard it said before that "Guilt says, I've made a mistake. But shame says, I am a mistake." This affect plagues many people raised in single parent households. Feelings of inadequacy and the absence of a healthy self-identity almost always produces feelings of shame. Shame is "a painful feeling of humiliation or distress caused by the consciousness of wrong or foolish behavior,"[14] or might I add, wrong or foolish thinking.

For a long time, my son believed he was the reason that his father and I weren't together. I think it effected the way he saw himself. When he was in third grade, his teacher Mrs. Kepler, pulled me to the side regarding his self-esteem. She stated, "He's probably one of the most popular kids in the whole school. People really like him." He attended a K-8th grade Montessori school and out of all the kids in the school, a third grader was one of the most popular. Where other kids saw him as a cool, popular kid, he didn't have the same perception of himself.

That's just like the devil... Always trying to distort the truth of God's Word. For, God said of all His creation, "It is very good!."[15] "God don't make no junk," as the old saying goes. We just have to believe the truth of who God says we are. We have to refute the lies of the enemy.

Not having a healthy self-identity affects all of our relationships and hinders a mighty move of God in our lives. God never sets us up to fail. He always "causes us to triumph in Christ Jesus."[16] We have to know that when we hope in the Lord, we "will never be put to shame."[17]

Fear, guilt, condemnation and shame are all enemies to inclusive parenting and to the Children of God. They distort the truth of who we are in Christ Jesus. Parenting from a place of fear, guilt, shame and condemnation will never produce happy, healthy kids who love God. You have to know who you are in Christ Jesus.

Know Who You Are in Christ Jesus

The enemy is almost always the *inner me*! We are our worst critic and foe. We have what Joyce Meyer calls "Stinking Thinking." We have to be delivered from destructive mindsets and behaviors.

Some of the toughest times of my life occurred in my childhood. I remember being caught up in so many webs of negativity, feelings of hopelessness and helplessness. I was bullied, dealt with tons of rejection and mounds of peer pressure to be someone other than the person I wanted to be... I didn't know who I wanted to be... who God had created and called me to be.

God wants us free from fear, guilt, shame and condemnation. He wants us to love the person He created us to be. He "has come that we may have life more abundantly."[18] God wants us to be free *and* happy.

Freedom is about having faith in God and knowing who you are in Christ Jesus. The world, the ex and many, many others will tell you who they want you to be. Only who God says you are is important. You have to agree with God about who He says you are. He says you are:

- Created in the image and likeness of God (Genesis 1:27)

- Chosen by God (1 Peter 2:9)

- Children of God (1 John 3:2)

- Accepted by God (Romans 15:7)

- Forgiven by God (Ephesians 1:7)

- His workmanship, created in Christ Jesus for good works (Ephesians 2:10)

- Crucified with Christ and no longer a slave to sin (Romans 6:6)

- A special treasure (Exodus 19:5)

- A friend of Jesus (John 15:15)

- Justified and redeemed by the Lord (Romans 3:24)

- A new creature in Christ Jesus (2 Corinthians 5:17)

- Blessed with every spiritual blessing in the Heavenly realm (Ephesians 1:3)

- More than conquerors through Christ who loves you (Romans 8:37)

You have to change your mind about who you are, your gifts and abilities as a parent, and about what you have been called to do. You must "be transformed by the renewing of your mind."[19]

The more time you spend with God, reading and studying His Word, praying, fasting and meditating on The Word... When you are quieted before the Lord, you are able to hear from and get to know God on a more intimate level and He shows you YOU.

God desires to have that intimate relationship with you. You can't effectively parent your kids on our own. You need the Lord's wisdom and guidance to destroy the yolks of bondage that exist in your life and the live of your children. The promises of God are yours and they are attainable. You have to receive them by faith and trust that God will bring them to past. He will!

Self- Care

This area of our lives is very important to God, for He desires that we are happy, healthy parents who love Him. We are not called to neglect ourselves for the sake of our children, or anyone else for that matter. We have an obligation to care for this temple that the Lord has blessed us with.

Self-Care is about recognizing when you need to rest, take a load off or just chill. It's about recognizing when you need to be refueled physically, emotionally and spiritually. Self-care is about getting what you need to be healthy and sane. Single parents must take extra precautions to care for themselves for we carry the load alone (that is with the help of the Lord, of course).

Self-care is best achieved in community with other people. If you are an extrovert, like me, a Girl's Night Out or a date might allow you to let your hair down and rejuvenate. I notice that I have more patience with my son when I'm allowed time to enjoy the company of other adults and when I am able to get time away from the home. Laughing and talking is so stimulating and therapeutic to me. I need it on a regular basis.

I remember a commercial where this man was babbling and talking gibberish because he'd been around his kids all day. I too, have felt like my vocabulary had been dummied down as a result of not having enough stimulating and intelligent conversations with adults.

If you are an introvert, you may need more time by yourself. Whatever relaxes you and allows you to rejuvenate, do that! It might be to get a babysitter for a few hours and check out a movie, go to dinner or snuggle on the couch with a good book and a glass of wine (one glass, lol). Whatever your pleasure, the objective is to make time to relax and rejuvenate.

The fifth commandment given by God to Moses for the Israelites was to "remember the Sabbath, to keep it holy." Sabbath means to rest.[20] The Scripture reads that "in six days the Lord made the heavens and the earth, the sea and all that is in them, but He rested on the seventh day. Therefore, the Lord blessed the Sabbath day and made it holy."[21] We have to learn the art of resting as modeled by God.

Our bodies need to regenerate. When we rest, it has a chance to do so. If we don't take the time to rest we become fatigued and maybe even ill as a result of us going nonstop. Our bodies can only take so much before it shuts down in an effort to reboot and refresh itself.

We can't run ourselves crazy all week- caring for the kids, working 40 hours a week, cooking, cleaning and the many other activities that we engage in, and not think our bodies will give out. We are "fearfully and wonderfully made,"[22] so much so that our bodies know how to make us rest. And we all agree that it's better if we slow ourselves down instead of our bodies shutting us down. Amen?!

There is a holy exchange that happens when we are obedient to God's commandment to rest. We are less frustrated and overwhelmed. When we are faithful to observe the Sabbath, by resting from our work, God blesses our endeavors. When we set aside time to honor God and our vessel, things become clearer and our lives, easier to manage. It's our way of letting go and letting God handle situations and circumstances beyond our control. Sabbathing requires very little from us, except to rest. The return (from God), however, is insurmountable. You'll find that God will work on your behalf in areas you could not have even imagined. For He can do the impossible.

Everyone can Sabbath. Be sure that your kids have food to eat on the day you set aside to rest and honor God. Talk to your kids about the importance of Sabbathing. Make that day a family day. Play board games, watch movies, read a novel together or allow everyone in the house to engage in their favorite pastime. Whatever you do, take a load off, enjoy each other and relish in the opportunity to honor God.

We are to Sabbath and we also need time away from our children. My girlfriends and I made a pact a few years ago that we would get together at least one Saturday out of the month to catch up with one another, go to dinner, a movie or simply for a Girl's Night In. We pulled names and vowed to bring a $20 gift for the friend whose name we pulled. We all listed several inexpensive items of things that we adore in an effort to bless and encourage one another.

We also vowed to travel together on vacation at least once a year. We've actually found time to travel more frequently than that, lol. We are all gainfully employed and great mothers to our children. We find it not robbery to treat ourselves from time to time and to enjoy the fruits of our labor.

If you are unable to get out of the house and away from your kids, you can still make time for yourself. Some nice and inexpensive ideas are to take a bubble bath every week. Grab some candles and some great smelling soap, cue your favorite playlist, and dim the lights to create your ultimate spa day. Let your kids know that you'll be off limits for a couple of hours. Set your boundaries and expectations of them and head to your private getaway.

Before I started going to the nail salon, I loved a great nail polish, still do actually. I still have a caboodle full of bright and colorful polishes. I would grab a new polish (for $1) just about every time I went in a beauty supply store. The vibrant colors made me happy and I loved to have my hands and feet looking good.

I would also pick up a magazine at the supermarket, or a good book. I like to read my news so, I would read news stories and articles online and surf the web. Surfing Pinterest, Facebook, Instagram and shopping sites have always been an enjoyable pastime for me. I also like to play games online. It's important for you to do whatever you like to do as long as your kids are safe and you are too.

I'm not much of a tea or coffee drinker, but most people are. You can create your favorite drink and designate a half hour or more as your quiet time when you need it. When my son was younger, he talked nonstop. It became annoying. LOL. Especially when he would go a hundred miles per hour as soon as we walked into the house from work and school. I just needed a moment. As a teacher, I just needed silence for a minute.

But, I didn't want him to feel neglected. So, I made a rule that when we came home we would allow twenty minutes of silence. I told him that I needed to use the restroom, change my clothes and gather my thoughts about what to cook for dinner. I told him that after the twenty minutes were up, he would have my undivided attention until he went to bed. We did that for a while. Hey, you have to be creative and do whatever you need to do to remain sane and to keep from hurting somebody, lol, including yourself.

There are plenty of ways for you to self-care. Just find what you like and make time to do it. You may have to put your kids to bed a little earlier, or you may have to pay a sitter to watch your kids for a few hours... or better yet, barter with them for their time. You may even need to wake up a little earlier to gather your thoughts for the day or to just enjoy the quiet before the storm. Just make time for peace and quiet so that you can relax and get your life.

Your family will not fall apart when you take time out for yourself. In fact, you will be affording them the opportunity to utilize *their* creativity and to actually play with and enjoy the hundreds of toys and things you've brought them over the years.

It's also imperative that you create a support system for your family. Someone to help you in your time of need. All single parents need outlets and support.

I saw a movie once where a group of mothers traded weekends, keeping each other's kids. I thought that was a great idea to ensure that they each had time for themselves. It might require that you tear down some barriers to allow others to care for your child. It will also require that you be willing to open up your home to other people's kids.

Identify who's on your team. Who is willing and able to assist when you need assistance? Can you schedule time for your child to connect with their other parent, and/or their family? Do you have grandparents willing to babysit or even transport a child to or from an evening event? Are there other parents who live nearby that could lend a helping hand? Establishing a community of support is imperative for all single parents.

God has not called us to go at this thing alone. We are at our best when we are in community with other people. Having an outlet... good friends and dependable family members are all necessary components for raising happy, healthy kids who love God. As difficult as it might be to believe, your kids appreciate time away from you, too, with your grumpy self. They look forward to you getting the help that you so desire so that you are more enjoyable at home. LOL.

Chapter 7: *Covering Your Children*

"For I know the plans I have for you, saith the Lord, plans to prosper you and not to harm you, to give you hope and a future."

Jeremiah 29:11

Psalm 127:3 reminds us that "children are a blessing and a gift from the Lord."₁ As with any gift that the Lord gives, we have a responsibility to nurture and protect it. In Matthew 25:14-30, Jesus shared a parable with His disciples on the importance of nurturing the gifts (or talents) that the Lord blesses us with.

The parable goes that the master gave one person five gifts (or talents), another two gifts, and a third, one gift. The one with five gifts doubled their investment, for a total of ten gifts. The second person also doubled their investment. The third person, on the other hand, misused their one gift and made no investment. That was considered an abomination unto God. The master rewarded the two who doubled their investments, but the other He condemned. This parable symbolizes the importance of making good investments with the gifts God gives. We can be parents who make good investments into the lives of our children.

Being fully engaged and proactive in our children's lives while they are young is so important because there will soon come a time when our children will leave the nest. They will go on to accomplish all the wonderful things that the Lord has called them to do. When that time comes, we want to be sure that they are nurtured and equipped mind, body, soul, and spirit.

A.S.S.E.S.Sᴛᴍ (Multi-Layered Child Assessments)

I will never forget the end of my son's sophomore year in high school. He had made some really poor decisions and I was an emotional wreck because of it. I was concerned that he would be leaving for college in a couple of years unprepared to venture out into 'real life' on his own. I prayed about it and asked the Lord to show me how I could help to better prepare him for where he was going, or rather, where the Lord was taking him.

I conducted an A.S.S.E.S.S.ᴛᴍment to determine his readiness for the real world. A.S.S.E.S.Sᴛᴍ stands for academic, social, spiritual, emotional, self-esteem-worth-identity, and sustainability. I A.S.S.E.S.S.ᴛᴍed him in every area to get a baseline. Then, I put together a plan based off of his strengths and potential areas of growth, giftings and abilities, and his likes and dislikes. I purposed in my mind to change his course of action and put him on a more productive path toward being all that God called him to be.

Although he needed to make some changes, I didn't want to crush his spirit in the process. So, I had to be strategic in my parenting methodology. I didn't want to come at him like "you need to change this and this in order to do this" so I decided to find one area to focus on at a time. I concluded that focusing on his spiritual growth would be the area that I'd get the most bang for my buck, so to speak. I thought, 'if he grew more spiritually, we'd see growth in the other areas of his life, too.' I wanted him to know more about who he is in Christ Jesus. That, I knew, would increase his self-esteem and confidence as it sets the foundation for everything else going forward. If he knows who he is, I thought, he can do anything he sets his mind on doing.

Now, I knew that I couldn't make Jai have a *personal relationship* with Jesus Christ, but I figured I could at least orchestrate (there's that manipulation again) some of his interactions and experiences to better condition his faith. I made a couple of huge changes as it pertained to his education and our place of worship. I enrolled him in a Christian School and we went back to our home church as I was preparing to pastor. It was very important to me that Jai be around other Christian families whose values, morals and goals for their children somewhat mirrored my own.

Changing his school was a tough decision to make. I was very troubled in my mind trying to figure out how I would make the transition comfortable for him. For, he would be leaving his friends he'd grown up with and there was going to be a serious culture shock at the new school, if you know what I mean. He was basically transitioning into the Fresh Prince of Bel-Air. LOL. I knew it wouldn't be easy.

Being in ministry, I've always toyed with the fact that I may not always be stationary and have to relocate to serve God. My son and I have had numerous conversations about him going to other schools and living in other cities. He was always pretty much opened to the idea of relocating and changing schools. That is, until the time actually came, LOL. Then, he got nervous and unsure, even bucked a little... but anyways. We went ahead with the plan.

I knew that academically, my son could excel at the new school, for he's smart, personable, fun and quirky. People like him and think highly of him. He can master any objective that interests him. He's not afraid to try new things... and he's handsome with a contagious smile, for he looks just like me, by the way. LOL.

On the flip side, he's lazy... only child problems, I think, SMH. Growing up, I never had to tell him to do his homework after school. He would just come in and do it. However, if he got a C (and sometimes even a D or F) on an assignment and the teacher said he could redo it for extra credit, you could forget it. He didn't see the value in doing it again. To him, he had done the assignment and the teacher should be content with that, LOL. He was pretty much a one and done kind of dude. Drove me crazy! I knew every teacher-parent conference exactly what his teachers would say... "He's smart, but lazy."

It's important that we A.S.S.E.S.Sᴛᴍ the needs of our children during every stage of their lives. I have a cousin who when he was a toddler, we weren't sure if the boy was deaf/hard of hearing, autistic or just bad (a term of endearment in the black community, lol). He wasn't clearly articulating his wants and needs but instead appeared irritated and would ignore your commands. It was as if he just went about life doing things his way. After a few professional assessments, and a couple of interventions, they determined that he in fact was just a bad butt little boy, lol. He just didn't want to listen to anyone tell him to stop doing whatever it was that he wanted to do. Had there not been assessments and interventions, his behavior could have become problematic.

A major part of the professional assessment that he received included measuring his intelligence and skill level. Come to find out, he's above average with no learning or behavioral disabilities and we are all amazed at how sweet and lovable he has become. He's still running around not listening and doing what he wants to do, lol. But, if you get him to settle down for a few, you'll be impressed at just how smart the kid really is.

Assessing your children is very important at every stage of their lives. When you notice deficiencies, seek interventions. Regardless of your financial situation, there are organizations and agencies out there to help. But, you have to be proactive about doing your research and taking advantage of the opportunities that exist in your community.

Many people are too proud to get assistance and to reach out for help. I get it. We don't want people in our business nor do we want to show weakness, but everyone needs help from time to time. Good parents get their kids the help that they need.

Many kids enter kindergarten and first grade unprepared. They struggle with letter recognition, writing their names and reading basic sight words. Just taking a few minutes in the evening working with our kids to help them learn to count, write their names, identify colors and reading short books, makes a world of difference in their education. You'll be amazed at their readiness for learning and just how far and how quickly your child will succeed.

World-renowned psychologist Abraham Maslow introduced the world to his pivotal work describing the hierarchical needs everyone must have in order to achieve self-actualization or fulfillment in life. They are: Physiological, safety, belongingness and love, esteem, and self-actualization. These needs comprise three categories: Basic needs, Psychological needs and Self-fulfillment needs. See diagram below.[2]

Self-actualization: achieving one's full potential, including creative activities

Self-fulfillment needs

Esteem needs: prestige and feeling of accomplishment

Psychological needs

Belongingness and love needs: intimate relationships, friends

Safety needs: security, safety

Basic needs

Physiological needs: food, water, warmth, rest

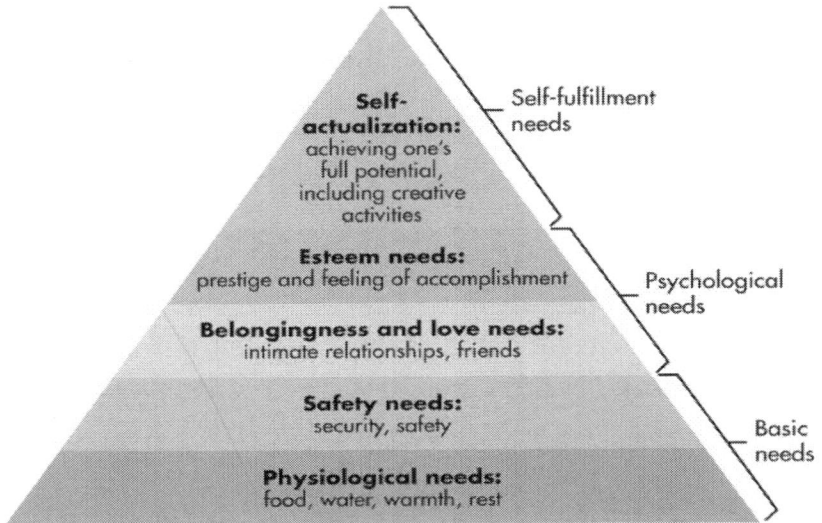

According to Maslow, if the basic physiological & psychological needs (located at the bottom of the pyramid) are not met, a child (or adult) will be unable to adequately progress to the self-fulfillment stage of life. In my twenty years as an educator, I, too, have found that when children's basic needs aren't met, they struggle with building and maintaining healthy relationships. They have a warped self-identity and many have learning deficiencies that hinder their capacity to achieve their greatest potential.

Years ago, there was a momentous debate around the wonder of nature vs. nurture and the impact they have on children. The question was, and still is today, which one is most instrumental at ensuring the success (or the lack thereof), of a person? Genetics or upbringing?

I don't know that that debate was ever truly resolved, or if we just concluded that they are both of equal significance. But, for the sake of my argument here, lol, I will say that although genetics is a powerful force in a person's life, it is possible to derail many of the harmful effects of genetics through proper nurturing.

We all have the same physical needs- food, shelter, clothing and security. Without these three basic and practical needs, it's almost impossible to reach self-fulfillment, or actualization, as Maslow coined it. As single parents, we may not always have a lot of money, but we can ensure that we are providing the basic needs for our children, for God promises to "supply all of our needs according to His riches in Christ Jesus."3

Healing Homes

Jesus told this parable in Matthew 7:24-27, "Anyone who listens to my teaching and follows it is wise, like a person who builds a house on solid rock. Though the rain comes in torrents and the floodwaters rise and the winds beat against that house, it won't collapse because it is built on the Rock (Jesus). But anyone who hears my teaching and doesn't obey it is foolish, like a person who builds a house on sand. When the rains and floods come and the winds beat against that house, it will collapse with a mighty crash."4

Your home is your sanctuary. It's where families are nurtured. It's where parents have the greatest influence and authority over what happens in their children's lives. Because we can't always monitor or control what happens when our children leave our homes, we are to take authority over what happens while they're there. We do this by cultivating healing homes, where love, communication and discipline rule. Cultivating an atmosphere of health and healing should be the priority for all single parents.

We can cultivate a healing home by monitoring our children's diet, their entertainment and social interactions in our homes. Healthy practices lead to generational blessings. Curses are destroyed when we choose to live healthy lives. This is why I believe nurture is more impactful than genetics. We can alter the harmful effects of genetics by empowering ourselves with wellness.

As an educator, I've seen many children come to school with bags of Takis, hot chips, candy, sodas and other artificial, sugary snacks and drinks. Some students opt out of eating the school's lunch (which is in *some* ways healthier than snacks) for unhealthy snacks. Students who have poor eating habits are more academically challenged and have a harder time staying focused in school. They tend to have more behavioral issues, too. Although there are many factors that contribute to low academic and behavioral performance in schools, the bulk of it, I believe, stems from a lack of proper nourishment and a lack of nurturing. We have to take authority over our children's health.

I'll be the first to admit that eating healthy is not always easy or cost effective. I know firsthand how difficult it can be to have worked all day at a stressful job only to come home to an even more demanding family who will not be denied. So, it's easy to order Chinese, stop at Taco Bell, or to order a pizza instead of cooking a healthy, time-consuming meal at home. But, it's essential for our children's health (and ours) to limit the amount of times we eat out in a week. It's also cost-efficient to cook our meals at home.

As a single mother, it was imperative that I budget fairly well. It's something that I've gotten more comfortable doing in my forties. When I made budgeting a priority and looked at how I was spending my money, I noticed that I was basically eating up all of my money. Which explains these few extra pounds I'm carrying LOL. I would go to the store, spend a bunch of money on groceries only to cook a portion of what I bought. When I did cook, I prepared too much and ended up throwing food away because we really didn't eat a lot of leftovers. Plus, depending on the activities of the week, I'd be too exhausted to cook anyway. So, we'd end up eating out. "What a wretched (wo)man I am... lol... who will free me from this body of sin and death?!"5 It was problematic and if I'd be honest, I still struggle in this area some days.

I realized that I needed to tighten up a bit and limit my frivolous spending and splurging. Balance is key! It was helpful for me to plan our weekly meals around our activities. If I knew that Tuesdays and Thursdays were super busy days, I'd cook something on Monday and Wednesday that could stretch on the days where time was of the essence... something I knew we wouldn't mind eating as leftovers... like spaghetti. There were some weeks when I wouldn't spend as much money at the grocery store because I knew there would be some long evenings that would prohibit me from cooking. Instead, I sat aside money to eat out on those days, or I'd grab a rotisserie chicken or something from the store and warm up a side of veggies. We have to find what works best for our families.

God revealed to me that there is a spiritual connection between parenting happy, healthy kids who love God and cooking healthy delicious foods for our families. The preparation that goes into cooking a healthy home cooked meal speaks volumes of the depths of our love for our children. Healthy home cooked meals not only provide sustenance for our bodies but also our brain.

Without all the preservatives, sugars and fats found in most fast foods, our children are clearer and sharper intellectually, especially when problem-solving. They're less moody and cranky. They perform better at school. They are happier people and more tolerable.

It can also be a fun experience to cook some of those meals together with your children. When is the last time your family cooked dinner together? If your children are anything like mine, they may have an attitude and complain about having to cook. But, I make mine do it anyway, LOL. He might get mad but he gets over it. In fact, it always ends up being an enjoyable experience for the both of us.

Every now and then we have to break the monotony that many of our kids feel about life. They need to know that they can enjoy some other experiences outside of being on their cell phones, playing their video games and hanging in the streets. We have to remind them that spending 30 minutes to an hour with their parents, every once in a while, won't kill them... because they think it will.

Cooking and eating together is healing. Sitting down at the dinner table is rewarding and benefits the whole family. It's a way to catch up on what's going on in each other's life and an opportunity to simply enjoy each other's company. You may be surprised at just how powerful this short amount of time can be.

It's very important to spend time fellowshipping with the people you love. Even Jesus, right before going to the cross, supped with His disciples.[6] Surely, we can find time to fellowship and to sup with our kids, whom we love so much.

Exercise is important too. My son loves basketball. I too, like to shoot around and play ball. So, we sometimes go together to a park or the YMCA and shoot baskets. I also like volleyball, tennis, softball and kickball. It's not often that I pass up an opportunity to participate in these sports, especially with my son.

Single parents may not always have time and/or money to subscribe to a gym. So, just grabbing the kids and going for a walk around the neighborhood or riding bikes has great benefits. It allows us to engage with the people around us while getting exercise and enjoying God's great creation. I've found that it's usually in the leisure, unplanned times that God does His greatest work. Something interesting might happen, we might engage in conversation with other people. We might even stop to join a game of basketball. Just a simple stroll is a great opportunity to bond with your children and your community.

It was an eye-opening experience for me the day I realized that I didn't have to have a lot of money or resources in order to engage with my son and to single parent him well. I only needed wisdom, understanding, compassion and love.

Maybe you don't live in the safest area and walking in the neighborhood is not a great idea. Try finding a location near your house that's safer, carry a ball and/or a baseball bat and play a few games with your children. We have to get moving somehow. Sitting around the house all day is not productive for anyone.

Please note that I am in no way trying to tell people how to raise their kids or conduct their households. My only objective here is to give a few simple and practical ideas to help enrich your family life and to give tools so that you can live the abundant life God promised you.

Establishing healing homes is about understanding the needs of your children. Teenage boys need to work. They need communication skills and work experience. They need to know how to conduct themselves in various situations and to problem solve. This is very important if they are to lead successful lives. If we don't embed a lifestyle of hard work and discipline into them, they will find themselves in trouble.

They also need to know how to maintain healthy relationships with their peers. They need good social skills. They need to know that it's ok to be nice and to treat a young lady with respect.

When boys are young, they can be learning how to work with their hands as well as their minds. They could cut the grass, change a lightbulb, wash the car and fix some things around the house. If you buy appliances or small furniture pieces, allow them to read the directions and assemble the parts. Learning to follow directions is a wonderful skill that they need to master. Plus, it's productive and keeps them off the streets.

Boys also need a good strong, male support system to increase their self-esteem, self-worth and to help them overcome the many pressures and adversities of life. They need to know how to set realistic goals for themselves. If the fathers aren't around, kids could get involved in sports and other extra-curricular activities where men are present. In many cities there are organizations like the Boys & Girls Club, Boy Scouts of America, YMCA programs, sporting teams, community centers and other programs that provide social, emotional and academic support for children.

I kept my son active with an organization called Center for Leadership Development. He completed programs like Project MR (Male Responsibility) and Jr. Self-Discovery. The tuition for those programs were either free or very minimal in costs. From those programs he was sought out to participate in other programs like IDEAA and the 100 Black Men Beautillion Militaire program for college scholarship money.

There are numerous programs available in our communities that aide in keeping kids off the street while teaching them valuable lessons about life. Some programs allow kids the opportunity to make money while learning a trade. God has sent these resources for single parents. It's our obligation to take advantage of them.

Girls need positive role models, too. They need to see and be raised by confident women... Women who are healed of their past and who have a positive self-image. They need to respect the women who raise them. They also need a male figure who won't abuse or take advantage of them, but who will remind them of their beauty and value. They need parents and loved ones to tell them they are brilliant and loved, because girls seek attention and love. They want to be the apple of someone's eye.

I was blessed many years ago to create a character education program at an alternative school I taught at. Two classes a day, I would teach nothing but character lessons on respect, responsibility, integrity, peer pressure, self-respect and esteem, amongst other topics. Many days we discussed sex education, alcohol and drug use and prevention, as they were the most engaging topics for mostly all of my students. I would tell them that no topic was off limit (but with respect and boundaries) because I really wanted them to have a safe place to talk, think through and reason about the many tough situations and circumstances that they had already experienced or could later encounter. I wanted them to be prepared for life.

I remember one particular lesson focused on respecting yourself and your body (it ended up being a sex education lesson, lol). The girls were shocked to learn that many boys don't have to have an emotional connection with the girl in order to have sex with them. Girls, on the other hand, usually likes the boy that she has sex with. That opened the door for more conversations on ways that girls could protect their positive self-image and esteem... especially by practicing abstinence.

Girls need to know that they don't have to give themselves away or put themselves on display in order to be loved. They are enough by themselves. Who God created them to be is perfect enough. They need to know that modesty is still in style regardless of the negative self- image and defilement that exists on the television and in pop culture. Girls should be raised knowing that they deserve love and respect from others, but more importantly, they need to love and respect themselves. They need to know that they are invaluable and they don't have to settle for less than God's best for them.

One thing that I really appreciate about my father was that he taught us how to do things for ourselves and to not have to depend on a man for anything. He said, "what if you don't have a husband? You'll need to know how to do this for yourself." My sister and I had to cut the grass, wash cars, change flat tires, you name it... My father didn't care if it was a male or female stereotyped-chore... you did it! As a single mother, I so respect this now as I'm able to get things done by myself and to teach my son these same basic principles.

All kids want to feel loved and accepted. Boys join gangs and hook up with the wrong crowd looking for love and acceptance. Girls often attach themselves to an abusive boyfriend thinking that the way he emotionally and physically responds to her is out of love and concern for her.

Wrong mindsets and stinking thinking plague us all from time to time. We have to see a lie for what it is and dispel it with the truth. The truth of God's Word.

Another important aspect of establishing a Healing Home is to monitor activities in the home. Being in ministry and conducting many events in my home, I've always been cognizant about the flow of activity in my home. I am the gatekeeper! I allow or disallow things to take place in my house.

I have been single since my son was about two years old. Although I have dated on occasion, I've never entertained an overnight guest in my home while my child was present. In fact, I've been celibate for the majority of his life and upbringing. God, I hope that changes soon, LOL.

I know that all single parents are not willing to make the sacrifice of denying their flesh as I've done, but we all can choose to control the interactions and influences in our homes. Too often we hear stories of mothers allowing men into their homes who molest and/or abuse their children. I don't know why that is, but I pray that you love yourself enough and your kids to deny access to anyone capable of doing those things to you or your children. We don't condone negative behaviors to get ahead or to be in relationship with an unworthy person. We have to learn to wait on God to send us mates who will love us and our children in the manner that we deserve.

One day I had a conversation with a friend about parenting. Our boys were very young at the time. She said that she does not keep alcohol in her home nor does she drink in front of her kids. I was taken aback, a bit, by that comment, but I really appreciated her logic. She said "if you don't want your kids to become alcoholics, don't have alcohol in your home. Whatever you don't want them to do, don't do around them." That struck a hard nerve with me and shortly afterwards, I kicked my nasty habit of smoking cigarettes. I literally said to my son one day, although he was only about three years old, lol, "Son, I don't want you to ever smoke cigarettes, so I'm going to stop." That day, I kicked that habit and haven't picked it back up since, glory to God! That's how generational curses are broken... Someone takes the initiative to change the trajectory of their family's lives by putting an end to destructive behaviors and mindsets.

It's only reasonable to think that what we allow our kids to experience and observe in our lives, and in our homes, is subconsciously telling them that it's ok and right for them to do the same things. To be aware of appropriate/acceptable vs. inappropriate/unacceptable behaviors is the antecedent to abundant living. We have to know that we are the most influential person in our children's lives. We are the thermostats, the gatekeepers and the parent! We have the power to break generational curses and to see to it that our families live the abundant life full of blessings and joy, that the Lord promised us.

Healing homes are peaceful homes established by God. They are able to withstand the storms of life because they're built on the truth of God's Word. They are filled with love and compassion instead of toxicity and frustration. Healing homes are harnessed with joy.

Healing Words
There are many memes and videos on social media portraying what it's like to be raised in an African American home. They are blunt and some are hilariously on point at depicting the African American experience. The most notable ones, I think, are the ones where a mother is disciplining her children and sometimes using profanity while doing so.

It seems that for most people, spanking and cussing go hand in hand, LOL, and I'm not going to condemn either as I've found that there's a time and place for everything. I will say that it's rare for me to use profanity, especially around my child, but not non-existent. I've been very intentional about what I say and how I say it, when I have felt compelled to cuss.

I'm raising a young man as a single mother. To keep from knocking him out, on occasion, I've had to settle for a few choice words. I'm not quick to haul off and hit him, so I need him to know when he's approaching the threshold of seeing his crazy mama in action, LOL, because I can go there. I call it putting the fear of God in him, LOL.

When it comes to physical discipline, or spankings, I've had to go that route a time or two as well. The Bible says "if you spare the rod, you spoil the child, but if you love him, you discipline him."[7] When children are young, you may have to tap their hands or spank their bottoms to correct them. However, spankings are an unproductive method for disciplining older kids. My son lost privileges when he misbehaved. He got his phone or video games taken away. He couldn't hang out with his friends or some other privilege was taken... whatever he really liked to do.

All kids need discipline. Parents, too, need it from time to time. Now, I am totally opposed to abuse of any kind. Parents need to be level headed when disciplining their children. You can't just physically or verbally take out your anger on your kids. That's not discipline. That's abuse and it's unacceptable, PERIOD!

Although I have used some choice words a time or two when disciplining my son, I also need you to know that I'm way more intentional about using words that heal instead of words that hurt. For "you can catch more flies with honey than you can with vinegar."

Growing up we would always say, "sticks and stones may break my bones, but words will never hurt me." I later learned that that's just a cliché we said to make the person doing the taunting to stop. We wanted them to know that their words weren't affecting us. When in fact, words do hurt. Probably more than any physical pain. Physical pain is temporary, but emotional scarring lasts a long time. No matter how much we try to downplay it, it can take years to fully recover from something someone has said to us or about us.

My mother once told me that when she was in middle school someone made a joke about her eyes being big and ugly. Since that day, as beautiful as she is, she has worn a bang. The kids taunting her made her believe that she had ugly eyes. She said it wasn't until she had a granddaughter with eyes like hers that she realized just how beautiful her own were.

That story baffled me, and everyone else who heard it. My mother is a very pretty woman and to hear her say that was mind-blowing. But, that's what happens. I've seen it plenty of times where children will come to school and act out if their hair is unkempt or undone. They'd rather be suspended than to endure the teasing of their peers because of their appearance.

We all take in so much negativity on a day-to-day basis that we all need a safe place to retreat. We all need someone who sees the good in us and who is willing to care enough and be tactful enough to build us up instead of tearing us down.

Proverbs 15:13 says, "a joyful heart makes the face cheerful, but by a painful heart the spirit is broken."[8] Parents and caregivers have the amazing opportunity of being that someone kids can always rely on as a source of strength and comfort... a safe haven, where they know they are accepted and loved and where their spirit can be renewed.

Kids are very delicate and have a hard time deciphering between what's true and acceptable and what's coming from a person filled with jealousy and malice. They take everything to heart. They believe everything. Parents have to tear down those strongholds of lies and deceit by constantly reassuring them of who they are... who you're raising them to be.

I often tell my son when he leaves the house to remember who you are and Who's you are... "Mine and God's," I say, LOL. I tell him he is "blessed and to not go out acting like someone unloved." In other words, "you better act like you've got some sense..." another black colloquial that you've probably seen on a meme.

Kids need to know that we have high, yet, reasonable expectations of them. When I taught in the classroom I would start the day by telling my students who they were and what they would accomplish that day. I'd tell them they were brilliant and had a bright future ahead of them. I also told them they were in the accelerated classroom, chosen because of their high ability. It was a stretch, but it worked! LOL.

When I called on a student to work a math problem on the board, I made them feel like they were the brightest student in the class, even the lowest achiever. I'd say, "You got this Dre'. That's an easy one for you!" Or, I'd say, "the people who wrote this problem think we're stupid, but we're smarter than that and can figure this out." And, they did. I used the same techniques at home with my son.

I don't know how it works, but showering kids (and other people) with positive affirmations help them to become great. They just need to know that someone believes in them and will not give up on them. That's how God treats us. He's always leading and guiding, correcting us when we're wrong and rewarding us when we're right. He places hope on the inside of us and it keeps us going, keeps us motivated and sustains us until we get where we're trying to go.

"(God's) love never fails. Never gives up. It never runs out on us."[9] He has good and positive thoughts about us. He's continuously luring us toward greatness. And, by this, we always win!

Kids need to hear, "you are beautiful" and " you are smart" and "you have something to offer of value or worth." It may be difficult to say those words if you aren't accustomed to hearing them yourself. So, you have to train yourself to speak life and only good, positive things about yourself and your kids.

A common practice in Antiquity, and still prevalent in many cultures today, is the blessing of children. Often, in Scripture, you will see a father passing down the blessing to his son(s), mainly before he dies. We also see the impact that the blessing has on their children. They go on to live pretty productive lives, for the seed of the righteous is blessed.[10]

Blessings are so important and all parents can and should speak blessings into their children's lives. You must tell them that they will be great and do great things. Remind them that the blessing of God is on their life and that He has an awesome plan for them. Whatever you want to see in your child, speak those things. Speak blessings and not curses, for you will see what you say.

Raising happy, healthy kids who love God is attainable when children have a healthy self-esteem and self-worth.

Parents create the foundation as either healthy and strong or weak and fragile with their words, as words have power. James 3:7-10 states, "All kinds of animals, birds, reptiles and sea creatures are being tamed and have been tamed by mankind, but no human being can tame the tongue. It is a restless evil, full of deadly poison. With the tongue we praise our Lord and Father, and with it we curse human beings, who have been made in God's likeness. Out of the same mouth come praise and cursing. My brothers and sisters, this should not be."11

You can fill up your kid's confidence capacity or crush it. If you want your kids to be happy, healthy kids who love God, focus on the former. If you want to live the abundant life God has for you, speak life because it's difficult for kids to love God when their own parents are hateful and critical toward them. It's hard for kids to believe that God cares about them, when the ones they love and depend on constantly crush their spirit.

Godly wisdom and compassion is what we need, for we do not always know which way to go or how to accomplish a thing... but, God does! We can ask Him for help in this area. James 1:5 assures us that "if you need wisdom, ask your generous God, and He will give it to you. He will not rebuke you for asking."12

Healing the Soul
The soul is made up of our mind, will, intellect and emotions. It's who we are- our personality, our desires, our appetite, our drive and ambitions. The soul weighs and processes our experiences. It manipulates our responses and behaviors.

Parents have a challenging yet amazing opportunity to shape those thought processes and nurture a healthy soul in our children. Although we can't change who they are, we can affirm right decisions, behaviors and emotions while challenging negative ones. If intentional, we can become parent-therapists, in our own little way.

I remember when I first got an understanding of why "soul music" is called soul music. It speaks to the longings, the disappointments and the burdens of one's heart. It resonates with our experiences of love and loss. Soul music touches the heart and pierces the soul. That is why, at some point in your life, you may have found yourself wanting a cigarette or needing a drink to endure the pain of love and loss that you experienced listening to the lyrics of a song. Usher's "Burn" has that effect on me. Having experienced love and loss and having to let go of love that I desired, that song really puts me in a funk... But, I love it! LOL. Soul music has the propensity to spark strong emotions and memories of something near and dear to our hearts.

What touches the heart or soul can ultimately influence the way we act and think. For instance, if we were hurt in the past, maybe by a spouse or a cheating boyfriend or girlfriend, when situations arise that look familiar, it triggers those feelings that we once had and we could find ourselves responding in the same manner as we did before. We can even place barriers where they're unwarranted, because we're afraid of getting hurt again. What we think is happening, we try to prevent and end up sabotaging what could be a really good thing for us.

We respond to situations and circumstances based off of our prior knowledge and experiences, even if there's no real threat or validity to the claim. Our thought processes just take us there. Our emotions and actions are driven by our thought processes, whether truthful or not.

I once saw a meme that said, "when kids don't answer their parent's call, parents think this has happened to their children:" (1) car turned over in a ditch, (2) kidnapped, (3) in jail, or (4) dead. As silly as it sounds, our minds do travel wherever our emotions lead, and it's usually to a negative state. We think for sure our kids are in trouble when in fact they're just ignoring the crap out of us. LOL. We think those negative thoughts because they are rooted in our souls. Subconsciously and even consciously, we worry about or fear the possibility of these things happening to our children. Our mind has a way of conjuring up scenarios to feed our fears and doubts. It happens to us all.

However, we don't have to be led by our fears and doubts. We can faith our fears and starve our doubts. We can teach our children to do the same. One way is by encouraging our kids to healthily rationalize their experiences as being different from someone else's experience.

My son loves to listen to music. Now, he uses AirPods to listen to his music, but as a child, when he got in my car, he would change the radio station from gospel music to rap music. When I allowed him to do so, I would noticed that some songs pierced his heart the way *Burn* did mine. I observed the music taking him to a place of wonder and imagination, LOL. I noticed (when I carefully listened to the lyrics), that they were talking about experiences that didn't mirror my son's life.

I had to remind him that what they were rapping about was not synonymous with his life. He didn't have to fight or fend, or sell drugs or kill anyone for anything. Rather, he was blessed and could simply go before the Father in prayer concerning the things he desired. He could even ask me because I like to give good gifts, too.

I know some parents choose to totally restrict their children from listening to certain genres of music, watching certain television shows and limit video games and social media, too. I, too, am all for censoring what enters our kid's ear and eye gate. However, being in education for about 20 years, I have found that kids will somehow learn the latest dance moves and lyrics to all the popular songs, with or without our knowledge or approval. In fact, parents would be floored if they had any inkling of all the things kids are exposed to in schools.

A grave mistake that parents make is ignoring or downplaying the fact that their kids are interested in and even engaging in these behaviors. Trying to prohibit these life experiences verses censoring and using them as teachable moments is unproductive. Kids will have these worldly encounters and will need guidance to sensibly process their experiences. Otherwise the world, their peers and pop culture will dictate how they process them.

At best, parents can and should run alongside their children like the gazelle giving them the tools they need to survive, both legally and logically. Parents should share prior experiences and lessons learned from those experiences with their children. That way, they will know they are not alone and that you are there to help see them through. That's how we heal the soul. We let our kids know that we understand what they are going through, that we love them and that we will be there for them as long as we both shall live.

Healing the Spirit- Person

When I A.S.S.E.S.STMed my son, I decided to focus more on his spiritual growth than any other area of his life. It's my belief that when the spirit is healthy, all other aspects of one's life improve. The spirit is what connects us to God and other people. You may have heard someone say, "we have kindred spirits." That means they have things in common with another person.

When a loved one dies, some say that they sensed the presence or spirit of the person because whatever happened reminded them of something that person would say or do. We are recognized by the spirit we possess.[13] We may be known to have a sweet spirit, a gentle spirit, a loving-spirit and for some, an evil spirit. It's the energy we give off.

The spirit-person, I believe, is the most neglected aspect of one's being, yet the most beneficial. Seems fewer people invest now-a-days in nurturing the spirit-person. Church attendance has significantly declined over the years as more and more families place a far greater emphasis on sports and entertainment then Sunday worship. Building up the spirit-person is invaluable if we are to heal our children and broken families.

Many kids are broken. They are mad at the world and no one seems to care enough to figure out why. Suspensions from schools and incarcerations have skyrocketed in the latter years. We hear of more instances of suicides and murders committed by children who claim to be victims of bullying.

There are a whole lot of angry kids in the world today. Sure, there are more who are leading happy, healthy lives, but we can't forget about the ones who aren't. Someone has to see about them. Someone has to care. Many of these kids have experienced more trauma in their few years on earth than most people experience in a lifetime. They're broken and angry. They've not found a trusted and reliable adult to help them process their emotions and realities. That's why we've seen such an increase in the amount of violent crimes and abuse committed by young people. They don't know how to logically process their experiences and pain. Unless we intervene wholly and expeditiously we will lose a generation to violent crimes, incarcerations, suicide and death.

Kids need a moral compass. Something and someone who challenges their irrationality. They need to know that you can't stomp a person to death because you're offended. You can't go and shoot up a neighborhood or school because you feel disrespected. They need to know that life is valuable, including their own.

Kids need to know that there are repercussions for every negative behavior. There are consequences at school, work and sometimes even through the judicial system. There are also consequences from God. They should know that the consequences from the latter can be far worse than the former so they need to use wisdom when making decisions. "For the wages of sin is death, but the gift of God is eternal life through Christ Jesus."[14]

Kids need to know that there's a time and place for everything. They need boundaries. They need structure. "As for me and my house, we will serve the Lord."[15] God and church must be a priority if we are to raise happy, healthy kids who love God and to enjoy the abundant life that God promised us. Education must be a priority. Being a good person with Godly morals and standards are very important. So are friends, family and fun... much laughter and much fun. All of those components must be present in order to receive God's best for our lives.

Kids will lead happy, healthy lives when they have a healthy knowledge and reverential fear of God. One way to instill into our kids a healthy reverential fear of the Lord is by modeling forgiveness in the home. Everyone needs to learn how to forgive and move on. We can't hold onto bitterness and anger thinking that we will live happy, healthy lives. Unforgiveness causes dis-order and dis-ease, and it manifests itself through broken relationships, fits of rage, destruction and illness.

When children are mad and bitter and angry with God, it's usually because they are mad and bitter and angry with you, the parent. Children view God in the same light (or darkness) that they view you and/or the absent parent. For some, God is a figment of one's imagination because the earthly father is missing in action. For others, God is reclusive and distant. As a result, kids believe no one can relate to them and their experiences. For many, God is critical and condemning, always seeking to punish. These wrong mindsets about our Heavenly Father all stem from the interactions or lack thereof that kids have with their earthly fathers (or parents).

We have to make church a priority again so that our children will know how much God loves them and wants them to live the abundant life He's promised. We have to get back to sharing the Good News of Jesus Christ with our kids because Jesus is still "the answer for the world today!"[16] You can try to overcompensate for lack by buying things, extending privileges, etc. to your children, but the greatest gift you can give them is Jesus. They need to know Jesus for themselves. In church and hopefully in your home, they are introduced to Him.

Parents have an anointing to heal the spirit-person of their children. It starts by being honest with yourself and vulnerable enough to be honest with your kids. Sometimes, I have to tell my son, "you know, I'm praying about this area of my life because I don't want it to pose a problem in yours." I encourage him, also, to pray about the things he needs changed in his life.

I may even say, "pray for me about such and such because I'm struggling right now," or "I don't have it all figured out yet, but I'm praying about it." I need him to know that I don't have all the answers and my life is not perfect. I'm still flawed, although I'm still cute, LOL. God is still working on me and I'm yet trusting Him.

This takes a lot of vulnerability because it shows our kids that we, too, are weak and fallible and sometimes find ourselves in a bind. It also teaches them that we know Who to rely on when life is tough. That's how we heal the spirit-person... by being honest, because ultimately, it's only by the Grace of God that we are able to make it through our own trials and tribulations. We have to put our trust in God. They need to do so, too.

I say to my son a lot, "you're going to have to do this for yourself one day... You will find yourself alone at times and you'll need your own relationship with the Father... Mom won't always be there, but God will." The older our kids get, the more they will trust and appreciate this invaluable gem you've given them in knowing Jesus for themselves.

One of my favorite Scriptures is found in Isaiah 61:1-3. It reads, "The Spirit of the Lord is upon me, because the Lord has anointed me to preach good news to the poor. He has sent me to bind up the brokenhearted, to proclaim freedom for the captives and release from darkness for the prisoners, to proclaim the year of the Lord's favor and the day of vengeance of our God, to comfort all who mourn and to provide for those who grieve in Zion—to bestow on them a crown of beauty instead of ashes, the oil of gladness instead of mourning, and a garment of praise instead of a spirit of despair."[17] The same anointing spoken of here is the same anointing we, too, can possess. We can heal the broken areas of our families. We can give our kids hope. We can set them up for a wonderful future. We can give them Jesus.

Chapter 8: *Called to Prayer*

"If My people who are called by My name would humble themselves and pray, seek My face and turn from their wicked ways then I will hear from Heaven, forgive their sins and heal their land."

2 Chronicles 7:14

It's impossible to raise happy, healthy kids who love God and to live the abundant life without having a decent prayer life. Prayer is simply communicating with God. It's emptying out your heart's cares, concerns and petitions before the Lord. Prayer is the vehicle to living the abundant life that God promised you. Everything you've ever desired and all that you want to accomplish can be obtained through prayer.

Having a personal relationship with the Father, through intimate time and prayer, ensures that we receive God's best for our lives. Matthew 6:6 says, "but when you pray, go into your room and shut the door and pray to your Father who is in secret. And your Father who sees in secret will reward you."[1]

I tried to come up with a fancy cliché or acronym for Prayer... For there are many, lol. But, what I believe God is saying to us is to simply pray! You don't have to get real deep and know a bunch of super spiritual verbiage. Just. Pray.

Prayers don't have to be long in order to be strong. Just. Pray. In Matthew 6:7, Jesus says, "And when you pray, do not heap up empty phrases as the Gentiles do, for they think that they will be heard for their many words."2 There's no need for a bunch of empty, useless words. God does not care about all of that. Just pray. For, there's so much power in your sincere, earnest prayer.

Set aside some time throughout the week to get alone with God and pray. Pray about everything that concerns you, because He cares. Ask for forgiveness for those things you've done that are unpleasing to God and even for those things you didn't do and should have. Prayer for others and yourself and don't forget to tell God what you desire. Most importantly, give thanks. "In all things, give thanks!"3

I've assembled a few prayers from my personal prayer journal that I use when praying for my family. Again, it's not imperative that you pray these specific prayers, but, rather you formulate your own prayer life and simply pray. It's my prayer that these prayers will aide you as you develop your own sincere and earnest prayer life.

Prayers of Salvation, the Blessing & Having a Personal Relationship with Jesus Christ:

Prayer: Lord, thank You for saving me and my children. I pray that we might draw closer to You and know You in the power of Your might and as our Lord and Savior (***Acts 16:31; Ephesians 6:10; James 4:8***).

Prayer: Lord, I ask You to free us from the chains of bondage and despair, bondage from rejection and divorce, bondage from peer pressure and trying to conform to this unjust society. I pray for release from fear & low self-esteem. I ask that love, forgiveness and a sound mind be ours, in Jesus' Name (***Isaiah 61; 2 Timothy 1:7***).

Prayer: Lord, when my children are down and depressed, teach them to pray. Help them to know that they are never alone. I pray that they know that You are with them and will see them through. May they never consider suicide, murder or even violence as a means of handling conflict and disputes. Let them find refuge and solace in Your Saving Grace and Mighty Power (***Psalm 23; Psalm 37:25; Proverbs 14:26***).

Prayer: Thank You, Lord for the calling that's on my children's lives. I thank and praise You that they are anointed and gifted to do Your Will. I thank You that they are walking in their anointing and gifting and that their gifts are making room for them and bringing them before great people (***Proverbs 18:16; Jeremiah 1:5; James 1:17***).

Prayer: Thank You Lord for allowing us to partake in abundance of the good fruit of the earth. I thank You that the blessing makes us rich and adds no sorrow. I pray we never despise the blessing, nor become wasteful of it (***Deuteronomy 6:11; Proverbs 10:22***).

Prayer: Lord, give my kids confidence and assurance in You and themselves that they might effectively grow to be all that You've called them to be. Help them to successfully transition throughout the stages of life. Give them knowledge, wisdom and understanding as they overcome the vicissitudes of life and to stand against the wiles of the evil one (*Luke 1:80; Ephesians 6:11*).

Prayer: Lord, help my children to be receptive to Your Word and teachings. Let us fellowship with one another in the peace and security that is ours through Christ Jesus. Let us worship together in the beauty of holiness and the Spirit of Truth (*Deuteronomy 11:19; Psalm 96:9; Hebrews 10:25*).

Prayer: Thank You, Father that our names are written in the Lamb's Book of Life. Thank You that nothing and no one can cancel the plans You have for our lives. Nothing can separate us from Your love. Thank You that our salvation is secure in You (*Matthew 19:14; Romans 8:38*).

Prayer: Lord, my children belong to You. God, I trust You to care for them, to lead and guide them, to protect and nurture them, to perform Your will and purpose for their lives. Thank You, Lord, for the blessing that's on their lives and that they are blessed and not cursed, all the days of their lives (*Deuteronomy 28; Mark 10:14-16*).

Prayer: Lord, I thank You that my children are saved and filled with the precious gift of the Holy Ghost. I pray that they live by the Spirit and not by their flesh. I pray that they are witnesses to Your salvation and bring many to know Christ (*Luke 10:21; Acts 19:2; Galatians 5:16*).

Prayer: Thank You, Lord for making us heirs and joint heirs with Christ Jesus. Thank You for not withholding good things from us. We are strengthened and prepared for life knowing that we have obtained the victory through Christ Jesus and have everything that we need (*Psalm 84:11; Romans 8:17; 1 Corinthians 15:57; Philippians 4:19*).

Prayers Concerning Child's Character & Behavior:

Prayer: God, create in _____ (insert child's name) a clean heart & renew the right spirit within him. Let his heart be pure before You and his actions to exemplify that pureness, in Jesus' Name (*Psalm 51:10; Proverbs 20:11*).

Prayer: Lord, help _____ to be open-minded and receptive to correction. Bring to their remembrance those things that I have taught them (am teaching them) so that it will be well with them. Help them to implement sound judgment and wisdom every day and in every situation (*Isaiah 3:10; John 14:26; Ephesians 5:15-16; Hebrews 12:6-11; James 1:5*).

Prayer: Lord, when my children fall or make mistakes, give them the confidence they need to get back up and dust themselves off by Your leading. Help them to forgive themselves and others. Teach them to let go and move forward (*Acts 2:21; 2 Corinthians 5:17; 1 John 1:9*).

Prayer: Lord, I pray that _____ not bring disgrace to himself or our family, but that they will remember who they are and Whose they are during times of testing, temptation, trials and suffering (***Exodus 20:12; Proverbs 29:15***).

Prayer: Lord, I'm not blinded to the fact that the enemy wants to sift my children like wheat, for that's his plan for us all. So, Lord I'm asking that they be equipped to handle life's adversities. Help them to resist the enemy so that he will flee. Help them to know to call on the name of Jesus, so they can be saved. I renounce pornography, abortion, drug addiction, alcoholism, sexual sins, lying, cheating, stealing and all generational curses that I have brought on and/or passed down to my children. I declare that my children are blessed and not given to generational curses. I declare that they will never have an addiction neither a criminal record. They will make good decisions. They are children of God and receive all spiritual blessings in Christ Jesus (***Deuteronomy 28; Galatians 3:13; James 4:7***).

Prayer: Lord, protect my children's self-esteem and self-worth. Help them to be confident in themselves. This world is so wicked and perverse. Help them to be certain of who they are and their purpose on the earth. Help them to be who you have created them to be. I pray that they are able to resist the enemy as it pertains to their flesh. I pray that they remain pure and confident until the appointed time of marriage. Lord, I pray that they will find the perfect spouse for them... one who loves and respects them... builds them up... supports them and who won't tear them down. Help them to remain faithful to you and each other so long as they both shall live (***Psalm 139:14; Jeremiah 29:11; 1 Corinthians 6:19; James 4:7***).

Prayer: Thank you, Lord for enabling my children to lead and be an example of Your love. Thank You for allowing them to walk in truth and in love every day of their lives. I thank you Lord that they are a witness and a testament to Your faithfulness and they share the Good News of Your Glory with others (***Romans 1:16; 1 Timothy 4:12; Titus 2:6-7***).

Prayer: Lord, I thank You that my children are the head of their class and not the tail, above and not beneath. I thank You Lord for giving them good success and that all is well with them all the days of their lives. Thank you for the favor that's on their lives for they are Your chosen vessels (***Deuteronomy 28; 1 Peter 2:9***).

Prayer: Lord, I pray that my children are respectful and obedient to their parents and elders. I pray that everyone charged with the upbringing and nurturing of my children will raise them in the way that they should go (***Exodus 20:12; Proverbs 22:6; Ephesians 6:1***).

Prayer: Lord, I pray my kids are never uncertain of my love for them. Any feelings of rejection I cast them into the lake of fire and declare that we are a family operating in love and by the fruit of the Spirit (***1 Corinthians 13; Galatians 5:22-23***).

Prayer: Lord, I ask that you will restore broken relationships within our family. Help my children to maintain a good relationship with their blended families and caretakers. Restore the hearts of the fathers back to the children according to Your Word. Let there be full support and resources to raise happy, healthy kids who love God (***Exodus 20:12; Malachi 4:6***).

Prayer for Children's Health & Safety:

Prayer: Lord, I thank you that my children are healthy and strong. I declare that no weapon formed against them will prosper. I thank you Lord that they are free of sickness and disease. I declare that their food choices are healthy and that they exercise to strengthen their bodies (***Isaiah 53:5; 54:17; 3 John 1:2***).

Prayer: Thank you Lord for my children. Thank you for allowing me to birth and to raise them. Lord, I thank you that they dwell in safety, peace and love, all the days of their lives. Thank you for given angels charge over them to protect them in all their ways. Thank you, Lord, for covering them and placing a hedge of protection around them, that no evil will befall them nor come into their presence (***Psalm 91; Isaiah 11:6; Jeremiah 1:5***).

Prayer: God, I pray that you protect my children's interactions. Let the people they encounter encourage them in righteousness. I pray that you show them favor and Your love through their acquaintances. I thank You that their friends are saved and serving You. Let them be drawn to righteousness, holiness and things that pertain to life and Godliness. I thank you that my children aren't drawn away by lust and easily swayed by temptation, but are able to resist the enemy on every hand. I decree that he has self-control (**2 Samuel 22:3-4; Proverbs 15:9; Isaiah 51:1; 2 Timothy 2:22; James 4:7**).

Prayer: Lord, I pray that You deliver my children from every attack from the enemy, in Jesus' Name (**2 Timothy 4:17-18**).

Prayers Concerning My Parenting:

Prayer: Lord, help me to make good decisions and to use sound judgment and Godly-wisdom when parenting my children (**Proverbs 22:6; Titus 1:5- 2:15**).

Prayer: Lord, I pray that I have the wisdom and confidence to discipline my kids according to the behavior warranted. For You said in your Word that if I discipline them, they will not die, but live (**Proverbs 2:6; 23:13**).

Prayer: Lord help me to speak life over my children (**Proverbs 18:21; John 10:10**).

Prayer: Give me discernment, Lord, so that I may comfort my children when needed. Guard my tongue so that I don't crush their spirit, but let my speech be gracious, always seasoned with salt, that I may win them over and establish confidence, healthy self-esteem, trust and acceptance. I pray that their father, too, provides the comfort and support that they need (**Isaiah 66:13, Malachi 4:6; Colossians 4:6**).

Prayer: Lord, restore the time that I have with my children. Let our days be filled with laughter and joy (*Genesis 21:6, Psalm 91:16, Joel 2:25; 1 Peter 1:8*).

Prayer: Thank you Lord, for trusting me with Your children. I know that I am blessed. I thank You for the blessing that's on their lives. Help me to be responsible with the blessing, in Jesus' name (*Deuteronomy 28:4; Proverbs 31:28; Isaiah 61:9; Luke 1:42*).

Prayer: Lord, give me patience and understanding with my children. Help me to encourage and not discourage them in any way. Help me to mother them as You parent Me. Help me to be obedient to Your Word. Help me to show compassion and love as they grow into adulthood and into themselves. Let me parent in truth and love and not from a place of brokenness (*Proverbs 14:29; Isaiah 61:1-3; 1 Corinthians 13:4; Ephesians 4:15, 6:4*).

Prayer: Lord, regardless of how the world moves and transforms, keep me consistent, persevering and steadfast in Your Word and in Your Love. Help me to keep Your laws, precepts and purpose at the forefront of my mind. Let me instill into my children what You have placed in me (*Deuteronomy 4:9*).

Prayer: Lord, thank You for my inheritance... that I will see my children's children... Help me to leave a lasting inheritance, one built on Your Word and Saving Grace. Help me to leave both a spiritual and financial inheritance that my children may be secure (*Psalm 119:11, 127:3; Proverbs 13:22; 17:6*).

Prayer: Lord, let my children's thoughts of me be admirable and filled with love. Help them to forgive me when I let them down, am critical or seem unfair. Let them always see the God in me and to have plenty of grace and mercy for me- a weak, broken vessel who relies on YOU for my daily portion (*Proverbs 31:28; Colossians 3:13*).

Prayer: Lord, I thank You that I am able to bless my children with good gifts. Help me to have balance, clarity and to use sound judgement and wisdom when parenting. Help me to not overindulge when I need to restrain (*Matthew 7:11; James 1:5*).

Prayer: Lord, increase my faith. Give me childlike faith so that my prayers be not hindered. Help me to trust You when I can't trace You. Help me to walk by faith and not by sight. Strengthen me to stand on Your Word in my time of need. Thank You, Father (*Psalm 119:11; Matthew 18:3; 2 Corinthians 5:7*).

Prayer: Lord, make me sensitive to hear the heart of my children- the cries of their heart, their joy and their pain. Let others hear my children and come along side me to raise them in the fear and admonition of the Lord. Help my children to feel loved and supported. Help them to know that their lives have significance and value and that they will make great contributions to society and in the kingdom of God (*Psalm 82:3; Jeremiah 29:11; Matthew 21:16*).

Prayer: Lord, let me not hinder the work You are doing in my children's lives (*Luke 18:16*).

Prayer: Lord, let not my parenting be exasperating to my children, but encouraging and strengthening, oh Lord, My Strength and My Redeemer (***Psalm 19:14; Ephesians 6:4; Colossians 3:20-21***).

Prayer: Lord, help me to get parenting right. I know that I won't be perfect, but I'm asking for Your Grace and Mercy to give it a great shot. Lord, give us a fresh start when we need it, letting go of all resentment and pain. Help us to start over with Your Grace and Mercy, each new day (***Lamentations 3:22-23; Ephesians 4:31-32; 1 John 4:18***).

Prayer: Lord, help me to manage my family well. Give me wisdom to bring my kids up in the fear, reverence and admonition of You. I pray that respect, trust, discipline, love and laughter fill my home and my family, in Jesus' Name (***Psalm 111:10; 1 Timothy 3:4***).

Prayer: Lord, I pray that you will send me a God-fearing mate to be my companion on this parenting journey. I pray they provide, protect and be priest of our home. Lord, I pray that they take great interest in my children's success and well-being. Let them fill the gaps in our lives with love, acceptance, understanding and Godly counsel (***Proverbs 18:22; Malachi 2:15; 1 Timothy 3:12***).

Chapter 9: *When it Looks Like You're Losing*

*"And we know that all things work together for the good of them that love Him and are **called** according to His purpose."*

Romans 8:28

I can promise you that it will not always look as if you're winning at single parenting. Even with much prayer, you may not immediately see the results you are praying for. We can plant seeds of righteousness and discipline our children and they may still veer off the path that we have chosen for them, to forge a path all their own. It's in those times that we must trust God all the more.

It's during those times that we must **pray for wisdom, understanding and guidance**. Proverbs 3:5 tells us to "trust in the Lord with all thine heart and lean not on your own understanding but in all your ways acknowledge Him and He will direct your path." God sees and knows all that our children are and will ever go through. He alone knows the path they should take. Parents have to do the best they can for their children and trust God to do what they can't.

It won't always be easy to trust God and to put everything in His Hands. For, if you're anything like me, you think no one else can love them like you do; no one else will care for them like you care. No one else has physically been there the way you have. No one has sacrificed like you. No one knows your children like you do.

It takes God reminding us that He loves them more. Our children are "God's workmanship, created in Christ Jesus for good works, which God prepared beforehand that (they) should walk in."[1] Yes, we love our children, but God loves them more. Yes, we have plans for our children but God's plan trumps ours. God knows what is needed to get our children where they need to be.

A single father that I know was experiencing some problems with his daughter. She was getting into fights at school, skipping classes, hanging with the wrong crowd and even found herself in trouble with the law. The father, embarrassed and outraged (as you can imagine) by his daughter's decisions and behaviors, couldn't prevent his daughter from hitting a brick wall. She ended up spending some time in a girl's detention center.

The courts determined that the daughter needed counseling because of her erratic behavior. While going through counseling, the therapist encouraged the girl to journal. It turns out the daughter found her niche while in this dark place and went on to become a therapist specializing in adolescence and trauma. From the looks of her troubled youthhood, it appeared that she would never be productive but only waste her life away. But, God had a plan for her. He allowed her to go through those dark times so that she could become all that He created her to be.

We never know who or what our kids will become. Had she not gone through those experiences, she may have never been in a place to passionately care for other girls and to help them overcome their trauma and to change their lives. God knows the path we should take and if we trust His leading, He'll direct our paths to that desired place in Him where we can find rest for our weary souls. He knows what's best for us... He really does!

We have to pray for understanding and guidance and then we have to **put on the whole armor of God.**2 Ephesians 6:10-18 reads:

10 Finally, my brethren (and sisters), be strong in the Lord and in the power of His might. 11 Put on the whole armor of God, that you may be able to stand against the wiles of the devil. 12 For we do not wrestle against flesh and blood, but against principalities, against powers, against the rulers of [c]the darkness of this age, against spiritual *hosts* of wickedness in heavenly *places.* 13 Therefore take up the whole armor of God, that you may be able to withstand in the evil day, and having done all, to stand.

14 Stand therefore, having girded your waist with truth, having put on the breastplate of righteousness, 15 and having shod your feet with the preparation of the gospel of peace; 16 above all, taking the shield of faith with which, you will be able to quench all the fiery darts of the wicked

one. 17 And take the helmet of salvation, and the sword of the Spirit, which is the word of God; 18 praying always with all prayer and supplication in the Spirit, being watchful to this end with all perseverance and supplication for all the saints."3

When things go wrong as they sometimes will, we have to remember where our help comes from. God promises to "never leave us nor forsake us."4 He promises to be with us come what may. The Call to Parent requires us to grow in our faith in God and to stand firm in the knowledge of Christ that "all things are working for our good."5

As stated in Ephesians 6, God has equipped us with weapons to use when we are under attack and when our children are under attack. We are called to stand in truth and righteousness, follow the way of peace, keep the faith, know that we are safe/saved, believe the Word of God and pray.

When my son was 16 years old, turning 17, (and while writing this book) he was diagnosed with Severe Idiopathic Aplastic Anemia. In short, bone marrow failure. His illness appeared suddenly and severely. There was no explanation as to why his bone marrow stopped working, it just did. This meant that his body was not producing the white blood cells he needed to fight infection, platelets, which prevent hemorrhaging, and his hemoglobin was low.

For months, Jai required blood and platelet transfusions. His ANC (Absolute Neutrophil Count, basically his immune system) was 0. He couldn't fight off any virus, fungal or bacterial infection. We would go home after a weeklong stay in the hospital, only to stay home one or two days, and then he would get a high fever again. Back to the hospital we would go. The doctors tried to treat and repair the bone marrow, but nothing worked. After two months, we decided we would go to Cincinnati, Ohio to prepare for a bone marrow transplant.

Of course, I'd prayed many prayers, many people were praying for us, even around the world. We fasted and sowed. But, this one particular prayer I fervently prayed: "God, it's very difficult for me to have faith at this time. But, at Your Word, I'm believing that we will see a miracle. God, I'm just really going to trust You. I don't want Jai to have a bone marrow transplant. I don't want him to have chemo. I don't want this sickness or anything like it to ever visit him again."

Three things I requested: (1) No BMT. (2) No Chemo. (3) Never sick like this again.

It took everything in me to constantly remind myself that I had prayed that prayer and I was determined to trust God. I would quote 1 John 5:14-15, "And this is the confidence that we have in Him, that, if we ask any thing according to His will, He hears us. And if we know that He hears us, whatsoever we ask, we know that we have the petitions that we desire of Him."

I would repeat, God I know You heard me.

We spent the latter weeks in December 2018 and the first week of January 2019 preparing for a bone marrow transplant; "the work-up" is what the medical team called it.

Chemotherapy was to begin on January 11, 2019 and the bone marrow transplant cell day was January 25, 2019.

Long story short, the week that Jai was to begin chemo, his bone marrow miraculously started to work. Two weeks later he was discharged from the hospital. No chemo! No BMT! And we're still declaring and believing by faith that he will make a full recovery and that no sickness of this magnitude will ever visit him again, according to Nahum 1:9!

I can honestly say, sometimes the way is still dim. Sometimes, I doubt and am afraid. I don't always know the end of a thing and how everything will work out. But, I'm learning to trust Him more and to rely on His Faithfulness and Wisdom to get me through. I have to remind myself that "many are the afflictions of the righteous, but the Lord delivers them out of them all."[6] God's teaching me, that no matter what I go through, He's got me.

He wants you to know that, too. So often we don't see God move in our situations because we don't surrender our situations and our will to Him. It's my hope that this book has inspired you to trust God more and to know that He loves you and your children. He has a great plan for your lives.

Not everyone's testimony will be the same, but we all will have a testimony about the same God, who is able to do "exceedingly, abundantly above all that we ask or think, according to the power that worketh in us."[7] When we invite Him into our lives *and* adverse situations, we will experience His Glory. We will see Him for ourselves.

God will show up in your situation. Have patience and wait on him. He will come through!

Above all else, when it looks like you're losing, **love deeper.** 1 Corinthians 13 gives us a blueprint on how to love and the outcome we can expect to receive when we do it. It reads, "Love suffers long *and* is kind; love does not envy; love does not parade itself, is not puffed up; 5 does not behave rudely, does not seek its own, is not provoked, thinks no evil; 6 does not rejoice in iniquity, but rejoices in the truth; 7 bears all things, believes all things, hopes all things, endures all things. 8 Love never fails."8

It's been said before that you can love the hell out of people and I believe it's true. A woman I know had a son who battled with drug addiction for a long time. He would be missing for months as he was on a binge and would pop back up after some time. When he showed back up, he'd bring a few of his buddies with him for he promised them that his mother would feed them and welcome them into her home. They could even shower and clean up if they needed to. On occasion they would spend the night.

Her family thought she was crazy to allow them to continue to come to her home, for there were numerous times when her things would come up missing. Although she didn't like that they sometimes stole from her, she loved the opportunity to spend time with her only son, to know that he was safe and to share the gospel of Jesus Christ with he and his friends. Besides, she told me that she had several storages full of furniture and household items, for every time someone close to her died, she inherited their things. She had multiple storages of things she never used.

She'd often say that her son and his friends needed someone, too, and she appreciated the opportunity to serve them, for that was what she felt Jesus would do. 1 Peter 4:8 says, "Above all, love one another dearly for love covers a multitude of sin."9Although her son eventually died from complications from his addiction, she's comforted with knowing that her son is resting with Jesus, as he gave his life to Christ before he died. Furthermore, some of her son's friends got clean and turned their lives around as a result of the love she showed them when they needed it most.

God has a way of making "all things work together for our good."10 It won't always feel good, nor will it always look good, but it will always work for our good.

Single parenting does not have to be a burdensome duty or responsibility, it's a CALLING! God has enabled, equipped and empowered us to effectively parent the children He's blessed us to raise. It's not an easy task, but it is a noble task... one deserving of honor and praise. When we strive to raise happy, healthy kids in the fear and admonition of God, we are indeed blessed.

When we allow God to utilize all of who we are... all of our experiences, our failures, our test and trials, God gets the Glory out of our lives. Our children are happy and healthy and we are able to enjoy the abundant life God has for us.

So, be encouraged in your parenting. Enjoy the call and the journey. Know that you are never alone. You are not without options, resources, resolutions and hope. Remove all doubt and discouragement for there are indeed two parents raising your children. You and God are a force to be reckoned with. God is faithful and He promises to be with you all the days of your life. Rest in that truth and watch God's Goodness explode in your life.

Epilogue:

As a single, divorced woman, I've always prayed for a spouse. I never imagined nor wanted to raise a child as a single mother. My vision for what a whole family should be, I thought, could not be attained by a single woman.

Since I began to write this book I've come to understand why God did not answer my prayers to remarry, when I prayed them. I've learned so much about who I am, Who God Is and what it means to find myself in Him. I've also gotten a rare opportunity to love someone unhindered and to the best of my ability. For that, I feel so blessed.

When God called me, I was at the lowest point in my life. I'd experienced so much loss and it was difficult for me to even trust that God was for me and had my best interest at heart. I'd been through so many things that I lacked the confidence I needed to do the things God called me to do. God Single Parented me until I started to believe in myself, or rather, the God in me.

I'm so proud of myself right now! God has enabled me to accomplish many things, but I believe that single parenting, writing about it and being able to share this with so many others is by far my greatest accomplishment. I

LOVE that I'm able to help so many others with this book. I LOVE that I am able to share the love of God with others and to provide strategies and be a resource to single parents. It's my hope that you feel the Grace of God covering your family as a result of having read my book.

This is only the beginning of what God is doing with the Called to Parent Series. For three years He has been downloading information to help me produce quality resources that will not only strengthen single parents and children, but families and communities.

For more information, visit my website www.calledtoparent.org.

1 Proverbs 22:6
1 Romans 7:24 (King James Version)
2 Ecclesiastes 1:9
3 Genesis 3
4 Genesis 3:6
5 Psalm 16:11
6 Genesis 4:2
7 Genesis 4
8 Genesis 4:4
9 Genesis 4:5
10 Genesis 4:8
11 Genesis 4:6-7 NIV
12 Romans 5:12
13 1 Corinthians 15:57
14 Genesis 17:5
15 Genesis 16:5
16 Genesis 16:6
17 Genesis 16:7-10
18 Genesis 16:10
19 Matthew 28:20
20 Romans 8:28
21 Genesis 18
22 Genesis 19:1
23 Genesis 19:5
24 https://www.dictionary.com/browse/sodom
25 Genesis 19:16
26 Genesis 19:17-26
27 Genesis 19:30-38
28 Genesis 19:36-38
29 1 Peter 4:8, NKJV
30 Genesis 25:23
31 Exodus 2:3 NIV
32 1 Samuel 13:14
33 2 Samuel 12:14-18
34 2 Samuel 13:2
35 Deuteronomy 5
36 1 Kings 4:31
37 Hosea 1:6-9
38 Hosea 2:4
39 Hosea 1:6-9
40 Hosea 2-3
41 Hosea 3:2

42 https://www.brainyquote.com/quotes/marcus_garvey_365148

43 (Guzik, Blue Letter Bible, 2008)

44 (Oxford University Press, 2018)

45 Matthew 1:19

46 Matthew 1:20-21

47 Matthew 18:10, ESV

1 Psalm 127: 3, NKJV

2 Psalm 127:1

3 Psalm 118:23

4 https://en.wikipedia.org/wiki/I_Am_a_Promise:_The_Children_of_Stanton_Elementary_School

5 Mark 8:29

6 Romans 8:28

7 1 Samuel 1:6

8 1 Samuel 1:11

9 https://en.wikipedia.org/wiki/Samuel

10 1 Samuel 3:4-6, NIV

11 https://lifehopeandtruth.com/prophecy/prophets/prophets-of-the-bible/samuel-the-prophet/minister

12 1 Samuel 25:1

13 1 Samuel 8

14 1 Samuel 15-16

15 1 Samuel 16:7

16 1 Samuel 16:11

17 1 Samuel 13:14

18 Luke 1:28-38

19 Luke 1:38, New Living Translation (NLT)

20 NIV

21 https://classroom.synonym.com/what-were-the-professions-of-the-twelve-apostles-12083577.html

22 Hebrews 13:8

23 Jeremiah 29:11

1 Genesis 9, Joshua 2, 2 Samuel 8

2 Deuteronomy 28:15-68

3 Leviticus 4:27

4 Hebrews 9:22

5 Galatians 3:13

6 John 19:30

7 Contemporary English Version (CEV)

8 Ibid

9 John 10:9

10 Proverbs 4:7

11 https://www.franklincovey.com/the-7-habits/habit-5.html

1 https://www.pewresearch.org/fact-tank/2018/04/27/about-one-third-of-u-s-children-are-living-with-an-unmarried-parent/
2 https://www.google.com/search?client=safari&rls=en&q=reclusive+meaning&ie=UTF-8&oe=UTF-8

3 https://www.imdb.com/title/tt0101507/

4 Malachi 2:13-16 (NIV)
5 Malachi 4:6
6 Revelation 5:8
7 Proverbs 22:6
8 Luke 5:16 NIV
9 Isaiah 40:31
10 Haggai 2:9
11 New King James Version (NKJV)
12 Luke 18:1-8 (NLT)
13 Hebrews 10:23
1 Isaiah 54:17
2 Deuteronomy 31:6
3 NKJV
4 https://en.wikipedia.org/wiki/Dear_Mama
5 NIV
6 Exodus 15:23
7 3 John 1:2
8 Mark 14:36
9 https://www.biblestudytools.com/dictionary/abba/
10 Matthew 27:46
11 Hebrews 12:6
12 Ephesians 6:12
13 KJV
14 John 3:16
15 Romans 8:17a
16 Romans 8:31
1 Proverbs 10:22
2 2 Timothy 1:7
3 Romans 8:28
4 https://dictionary.cambridge.org/us/dictionary/english/guilt
5 Romans 3:23
6 1 John 1:9
7 https://www.dictionary.com/browse/condemn
8 Jeremiah 29:11
9 https://peanuts.fandom.com/wiki/%22Pig-Pen%22
10 Zechariah 2:8

11 Matthew 10:31

12 Isaiah 61:3

13 2 Corinthians 12:9

14 Dictionary.Com Unabridged - Based On The Random House Unabridged Dictionary, © Random House, Inc. 2019

15 Genesis 1:31

16 2 Corinthian 2:14

17 Psalm 25:3

18 John 10:10

19 Romans 12:2

20 https://www.biblestudytools.com/dictionary/sabbath/

21 Exodus 20:8-11

22 Psalm 139:14

1 Contemporary English Version (CEV)

2 https://www.simplypsychology.org/maslow.html

3 Philippians 4:19

4 NLT

5 Romans 7:24

6 Matthew 26:17-30; Mark 14:12-26, Luke 22:7-39 and John 13:1-17:26

7 Proverbs 13:24

8 NET Bible

9 Song lyrics by Jesus Culture

10 Psalm 112:2

11 NIV

12 NLT

13 Matthew 7:20

14 Romans 6:23

15 Joshua 24:15

16 Andrae Crouch's "Jesus is the Answer"

17 NIV

1 ESV

2 Ibid.

3 1 Thessalonians 5:18

1 Ephesians 2:10

2 Ephesians 6:10-18

3 NKJV

4 Deuteronomy 31:6

5 Romans 8:28

6 Psalm 34:19

7 Ephesians 3:20

8 NKJV

9 NIV

10 Romans 8:28

Made in the USA
Lexington, KY
29 November 2019